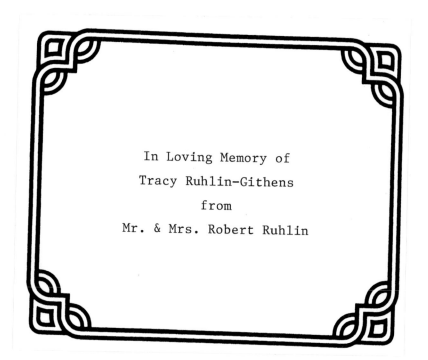

In Loving Memory of
Tracy Ruhlin-Githens
from
Mr. & Mrs. Robert Ruhlin

Colorful GARDENS

Colorful GARDENS

Contrast & Combine Your Plants & Flowers for Spectacular Visual Effects

Modeste Herwig

 Sterling Publishing Co., Inc. New York

Cover photo
**The soft colors
in this border
around a pond
are in har-
mony with
each other.**

This book has been written with meticulous care. Plant
heights and bloom times are determined by climate and soil
conditions. Data in the color tables cannot represent all hardiness zones. Check with a local nursery or garden supplier to
determine the potential for success of a specific plant in a
given hardiness zone.

Herwig, Modeste.
    [Kleurrijke tuinen. English]
    Colorful gardens : contrast & combine your plants & flowers for
spectacular visual effects / Modeste Herwig.
        p.   cm.
    Includes index.
    ISBN 0-8069-0625-1
    1. Color in gardening.   2. Gardens—Design.   I. Title.
SB454.3.C64H4713   1994
712'.2—dc20   93-43390
                                                          CIP

Translated by Karin Ford-Treep

Our thanks to Tony Dove, horticulturist of Tryon Palace, New Bern,
North Carolina, for his assistance with the color tables.

Library of Congress Cataloging-in-Publication Data

10   9   8   7   6   5   4   3   2   1

Published 1994 by Sterling Publishing Company, Inc.
387 Park Avenue South, New York, N.Y. 10016
Originally published and © 1992 by
Zomer en Keuning Boeken B.V., Ede
under the title *Kleurrijke Tuinen*
English translation © 1994 by Sterling Publishing Co., Inc.
Distributed in Canada by Sterling Publishing
% Canadian Manda Group, P.O. Box 920, Station U
Toronto, Ontario, Canada M8Z 5P9
Distributed in Great Britain and Europe by Cassell PLC
Villiers House, 41/47 Strand, London WC2N 5JE, England
Distributed in Australia by Capricorn Link (Australia) Pty Ltd.
P.O. Box 6651, Baulkham Hills, Business Centre, NSW 2153, Australia
Printed and Bound in China

Sterling ISBN 0-8069-0625-1

TABLE OF CONTENTS

Left
A wide border in yellow, violet, and white. Accents are provided by shrubs trimmed to rounded shapes, which are located among the perennials and also behind the border.

Right
In this border based on color, the greygreen leaves provide a restful base.

PREFACE

The atmosphere in a garden is to a large extent determined by the colors used in that garden. A conscious choice of colors will give your garden a very personal aura. *Colorful Gardens* shows you the possibilities that exist.

After an introduction about the various aspects of color, a chapter is devoted to each of the nine principal colors. For each color, attention is paid to the character of that color and to successful combinations with other colors. Included at the end of each chapter is a creative border design to get you started.

In this book about the use of color in gardens, my starting point has been the set of color cards published by the Royal Horticultural Society in cooperation with the Hollands Bloemenbureau, the Dutch Office for Flowers. The logical categorization and identification of the colors used in this system constitute the basis for the book. With the help of these color cards, my father, Rob Herwig, has planted marvellous borders based on color in the Model Gardens. Two of these borders have been included in this book, the yellow-white-grey border and the yellow-orange-red border. Working in the Model Gardens, I have used the color cards extensively over the last few years. Fascinated by the possibilities they afford for gardens, I began a more in-depth study of the color theory and, as a result, I undertook the writing of *Colorful Gardens*.

Knowledge of the color theory presented in the introduction is a great help in designing gardens based on color. But a feel for colors is very important as well. I hope this book will serve as a guideline for enthusiastic gardeners who want to design gardens consciously based on color.

Modeste Herwig

INTRODUCTION

Left
Purple *Centaurea dealbata* and violet horned violets.

A subtle color combination of the white and red-purple rose *Rosa* 'Rosa Mundi' with the light violet-blue crane's bill *Geranium pratense* "Mrs. Kendall Clark."

Colors have always been important to people. From the beginning of time they have been a means of indicating to others that we do or do not belong together. Colors are used as distinguishing marks of nations, communities, and individuals. This can be expressed by the national colors of a flag, the colors of clothing worn in religious or political communities and in the clothing, interior design, and various art forms—including gardening—closen by individuals.

Everything has color, and the colors that surround us influence our emotions, even though we may scarcely be aware of it. Or, to use the words of the painter Kandinsky, colors exert a direct influence on our souls. Red, for example, makes us more active. Someone who is exposed to red light or who sits in a red room will have higher blood pressure and will breathe faster, while experiencing a rise in body temperature. When exposed to green and blue light, the person's reactions will be the exact opposite. Hence the colors of interiors exert an influence on us, as do the colors of gardens, our clothing, or the products we buy.

Colors also have important symbolic meanings and we can (without being aware of it) express our emotions by means of color. Carl Jung was one of those who studied this phenomenon, and colors are still used in various psychological therapies.

Unfortunately, colors play a secondary role for many people. They consider colors a matter of course and often do not really look at them. This despite the fact that some two hundred colors can be distinguished in the color spectrum. These can be mixed to a greater or lesser extent, producing a number of possibilities that is almost limitless. Human beings can distinguish about one million different shades! A color meter can even measure some nine million different ones. We can develop our ability to see colors by consciously looking at the colors around us. There is much to be enjoyed! And this is certainly the case with the colors that can be admired in gardens.

9

A COLORFUL HISTORY

The First Ornamental Gardens

There is a growing interest today in the application of consciously chosen colors to a garden. But it was not always this way! Originally, gardens only served a useful purpose and colors played a secondary role. Ornamental gardens were designed as soon as an appropriate opportunity arose. They were created as pleasure gardens, as places of relaxation, and as places where the beauty of nature could be enjoyed.

The first gardens probably appeared in ancient Sumer; and there were ornamental gardens as well in ancient Egypt, China, Japan, Greece, and in the Roman Empire. In Europe, it began with the convents, which had gardens that were mainly used for the cultivation of herbs. For practical purposes, the plants were placed in neat beds with straight lines, generally laid out in a symmetrical arrangement. This concept was transferred to ornamental gardens and this unnatural layout with straight lines continued for a very long time. In this type of arrangement, both in the Renaissance gardens and in the ornamental beds of the Baroque gardens, the plants themselves were less important than the design. Examples can still be seen at Versailles and at the Het Loo palace near the Dutch city of Apeldoorn. There was no conscious use of color in these ornamental gardens.

Garden Designers Show Their Colors

In England, early in the Eighteenth Century, people were beginning to request gardens with a more natural design allowing for more room for the plants. The selection of plants was also increasing since a great many new ones were being introduced by way of the botanical gardens.

The art of gardening in England was greatly influenced by Gertrude Jekyll, who had studied art before becoming involved with gardens. She decided that the concepts she had learned in the various color theories were also appropriate for use in her designs for gardens. Gertrude Jekyll painted, so to speak, with the colors of the plants and she might therefore be called the first Impressionist gardener. Various color combinations were discussed in *Colour in the Flower Garden*, a book published in 1908 (as of 1914, the title has been *Colour Schemes for the Flower Garden*). Her use of contrasts was much stronger than is customary today and everything was somewhat too cultivated, but color was the point of departure for her designs and that was indeed something new!

A formal garden with *Buxus* hedges cut in straight lines and forming a symmetrical pattern. Shape is more important than color in this garden.

Monet's garden in Giverny, with the painter's house in the background.

Gardening with colors continued to develop, and the British became masters in the design of borders based on the colors of the plants. Splendid examples are the famous gardens of Vita Sackville-West surrounding Sissinghurst castle in Kent. I still feel nostalgia for these gardens that are so full of atmosphere.

Several other books have also appeared in England about the use of color in gardens, for example, *Colour in Your Garden* by Penelope Hobhouse.

In France, the Impressionist painter Monet expressed his ideas about color in the design of the garden around his house at Giverny starting in 1883. He was especially fascinated by the effect of light on colors. He discovered that, in the cool light of morning, the garden's colors looked very different from the way they did when the plants were exposed to the bright, warm light of the sun. He captured these differences in color in scores of beautiful paintings. His garden has now been restored and opened to the public. In the Netherlands, the landscape gardener Mien Ruys has exerted considerable influence. In her designs, borders containing perennials play an important part. In Dutch gardens, much continues to be done with perennials, and there is a continuing interest in color. A Dutch book has even been published that deals exclusively with blue flowers, *Blauwe bloemen* (Blue Flowers), by R. Leopold and R. Verel. Specialized nurserymen obtain plants from abroad or breed new forms themselves, thus producing a very large selection. This is important, of course, because plants are the medium of garden artists. Using plants, they can make sophisticated combinations of color that determine the atmosphere of the garden. Examples of gardens designed for color can be seen in several gardens in the Netherlands that are open to the public, such as the gardens of Ton ter Linden in Ruinen and the Rob Herwig Model Gardens in Lunteren. Much is done with colors also in a number of famous private gardens in the province of Zeeland. These are open to the public for a few days every year. Like the photographs in this book, they may inspire you to turn your own garden into a work of art.

Right
The "Grey Walk" in Hestercombe Gardens, designed by the famous English landscape gardener Gertrude Jekyll.

COLOR IN THE WORLD OF PLANTS

Why Do Plants Have Color?

Before examining which aspects of the theory of color are useful in gardening, I first want to take a moment to ponder the reasons for color. Why do leaves, and especially flowers, have such splendid colors? Like everything in nature, colors have a function. Colors are part of life and they are important for the propagation of the species.

Leaves and Stems

In leaves and stems the pigment chlorophyll provides the green color, but it is also essential for the important process of photosynthesis. Aided by the energy obtained from the light of the sun, this process plays an important part in providing plants with nourishment. There are other pigments as well that contribute to the metabolism of plants. When there is some malfunction in the metabolism, a characteristic discoloring of the leaves is often seen. In potato plants, for example, brown leaves may indicate a lack of potassium. The red pigment anthocyanin has a protective function. Hence, as a protection against bright sunlight, many vulnerable young leaflets have a reddish color produced by this pigment when they first come out.

In autumn the chlorophyll is broken down and other pigments, such as carotenoids, are exposed to the light. They produce the red, orange, and yellow shades of color that can be seen in the splendid discolorations of the leaves in autumn.

Flowers Full of Fragrance and Color

The colors of flowers have a function in the propagation of plants. The colorful and often fragrant petals are signals. They entice the appropriate pollinator to the stamens and pistils so that fertilization can take place. The flower is, so to speak, the sign advertising the presence of nectar. Most insects are very sensitive to colors and have special preferences for specific shades of color. Honeybees can be "trained" to color signals; in fact, various types of tests have resulted in a considerable amount of knowledge about their vision. They see the world of flowers differently from the way we do. They do not see red, but they are very sensitive to ultraviolet, a color we cannot see. This is true of all the insects that have been tested. It affords insects an image that is often different from the one we see. For example, we see the color of the flower of the silverweed as pure yellow, while bees see a clearly defined dark, ultraviolet disk that indicates the entrance.

The tender young leaves of the "Lady Seton" rose are protected against the intense light of the sun by the pigment anthocyanin.

Colors are nature's smiles.

Leigh Hunt

14

Since insects do not see red, there are hardly any indigenous plants with red flowers in our geographical region. An exception is the bright red poppy; however, this flower is seen as ultraviolet by insects. Birds, on the other hand, are very sensitive to red. In fact, in America and Africa, red flowers are pollinated by hummingbirds! In the northern regions, many berries and other fruits are red in order to attract birds that will take care of propagating them.

To show insects, which are often somewhat nearsighted, the way to the nectar, petals sometimes have honey guides that serve as beacons. They are stripes, specks, or dots that mark the entrance. Even when we do not see anything special, ultraviolet signs are often present. Flowers that are pollinated by flies never have honey guides because they could not be seen by flies, which are mainly attracted by scents.

Beetles have poor vision. Hence, plants that depend on them for pollination always have large flowers, generally white and very fragrant (such as the magnolia), so that they are easy to identify. Flowers that are pollinated by moths also have light colors and strong fragrances so that they are easy to find in the dark. The advertising sign is simply adapted to the target group.

Sometimes color is even used to indicate whether or not a flower has already been visited by a pollinator, as in the case of the horse chestnut. The white flowers of this tree are marked with a yellow speck. However, as soon as pollination has taken place, the yellow turns red. This makes it invisible to bees; hence, it is a sign that the nectar is finished. The function of the colors that mark certain seeds and fruits when they are ripe is also to attract animals which will propagate them, as in the case of the red berries to which birds are drawn.

Pigments Provide Color

The color of plants is determined by the chemical composition of pigments and the structure of the surface. Important pigments that occur in plants are anthocyanins (purple, blue, and red), anthoxanthins (yellow), chlorophyll (green), carotenoids (orange), and xanthophyll (yellow). Many colors are the result of combinations of pigments. In addition, the structure of the surface gives character to the colors of the petals. For example, cells that contain amyloplasts convey gloss. Very fine hairs give flowers a velvety color; a thin layer of wax or a fatty surface makes them look glossy; even the arrangement of the cells may provide special effects.

Again, each of these elements has, of course, a specific function, such as limiting evaporation in the case of a thin layer of wax or very fine hairs.

White flowers sometimes have colorless petals that are filled with tiny air bubbles. These petals look white, just as colorless water turns white when it freezes. Try squeezing a petal of a snowdrop or white rose until the air escapes and you will see it become colorless and somewhat transparent.

There are other physical elements that may produce a white surface. Cream-colored flowers that are almost white in color do have a pigment; they owe their color to anthoxanthins.

COLOR THEORY AND THE ART OF GARDENING

There are, of course, people who have such a fantastic feeling for colors that they can devise the most beautiful color combinations without having any specific knowledge. But for everyone else who finds this somewhat difficult, it is useful to know something about color theories. We all have our favorite colors, but combining colors is often difficult. Colors do not stand alone, they are, in fact, influenced by surrounding colors. This phenomenon is discussed extensively in color theories and if we use this knowledge, we can obtain beautiful effects.

The Secret of Color

Through the ages, various people have been concerned with the question of how colors are generated. The ancient Greeks tried to learn the secrets of light and color. Leonardo da Vinci was fascinated by the phenomenon of color as well. It was only in 1666 that Newton discovered the secret of the spectrum when he let a ray of sunlight shine through a prism. Thus he separated light into the seven spectral colors: red, orange, yellow, green, blue, indigo (purple), and violet. Much later again, various color theories were formulated and elaborated. The poet Goethe devised a color circle with six colors. Chevreul, president of a dye-works for wall hangings, wanted to know more about the (undesired) effect of colors on each other in tapestries. The extensive color circle he invented comprised 14,400 shades! Johannes Itten, the great German painter and teacher of color theories at the well-known Bauhaus school, also taught much about color.

Light Is the Mother of All Colors

Colors are generated by light. Isn't it true that in the dark no colors can be distinguished? The seven colors of the spectrum are contained in a ray of (white) sunlight. When the light shines through a prism, the colors become visible. We can see the colors also in the brilliance of a diamond or a soap bubble, and in a rainbow. But what gives an object its one specific color?

In the 19th century, it was discovered that light is a phenomenon of waves comparable to other electromagnetic rays, such as X-rays, radar, radio, and television waves. In principle, such a wave motion looks like a cord that is moved back and forth at one end. The distance that a wave travels in one oscillation period is called the wavelength. This wavelength is very small for light, more or less one half millionth of a metre.

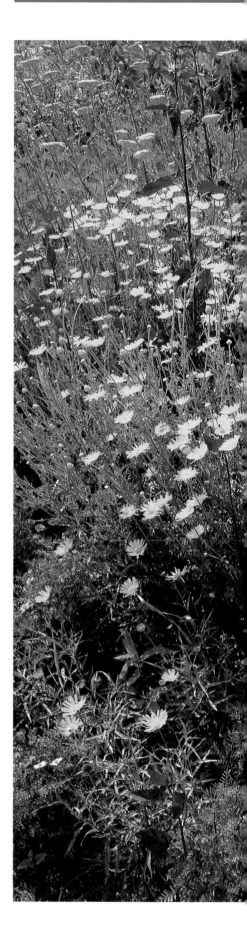

A beautiful combination of yellow and orange flowers, grey-green leaves, and leaves with a dark color in the gardens of Ton ter Linden.

Every color has its own wavelength. Colored objects absorb certain wavelengths of the light and reflect others. On their own, they do not have any color. Only the light that is *reflected* by the object is observed by us and seen as the color of the object. It is here that pigments play an important part. The pigments in the object determine which wavelengths are selected and, thus, they determine the colors. They are compositions that absorb only a limited part of the spectrum and reflect the remainder. In the case of a red flower, the pigments in the petals cause all the wavelengths of the light to be absorbed except the red light, which is reflected and gives the flower its red color. There are also objects that absorb practically all the light, making them look black; an example is black velvet, the blackest black there is. Objects that reflect all the light are white. In this case, the composition of the light does not change and hence it remains white. In the case of a grey object, all the wavelengths are absorbed equally, but a part are also reflected.

We can only observe the "real" color of objects when they are exposed to white light. When the light is colored, i.e., when it lacks certain parts of the spectrum, a totally different color results.

This principle can also be observed in the garden. The composition of sunlight differs with the time of day and with the weather; hence it influences the colors of the plants. In bright sunlight, a yellow glow pervades all colors. At the end of the day, there is more red light, which makes all colors redder. At that time, a bright red-purple rose will look redder. If we look at colors in a somewhat superficial manner, our eyes adjust and we always see the same colors, whatever the type of light. If we look very carefully, we can observe many differences during the course of the day.

Monet was so fascinated by these changes in color caused by the seasons, the time of day, and the changes in weather that he dedicated many beautiful studies to this phenomenon. He would choose a subject, such as a building, a haystack in the fields, or the water lilies in his pond, and make several paintings of it, each under different light conditions. He painted the cathedral of Rouen at least 40 times! In such a series, the colors of the individual paintings are completely different.

The Color Circle

Several different color circles have been devised in order to obtain a clear view of the arrangement of the colors. Most of the circles are composed of the primary colors red, yellow, and blue, which are the three basic colors that cannot be obtained by the mixing of other colors. In between these, are the colors that are produced when these colors are mixed. They are: orange (red mixed with yellow), green (yellow mixed with blue), and purple (blue mixed with red); these are the secondary colors. When these secondary colors are mixed again with the primary colors, tertiary colors such as blue-green and red-purple will be produced.

The pure colors of the circle symbolize in a way the many color gradations that we see around us. Thus, red represents all the reddish hues, green all the greens. The clear and rigid division is artificial but extremely

Top left
A photo of the virgin's bower *Clematis integrifolia* taken on a cloudy day.

Bottom left
The same photo, but now taken on a sunny day. There is more yellow in the light now, so the leaves become yellow-green and the flowers somewhat more purple.

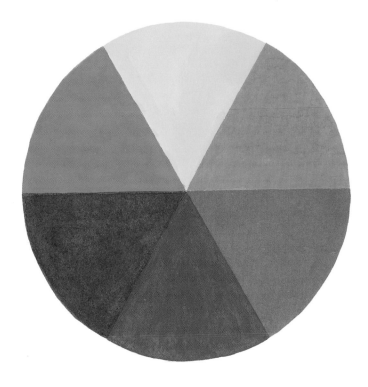

A simple color circle, consisting of the primary colors red, yellow, and blue, as well as the secondary colors orange, green, and purple.

21

helpful when choosing color combinations. Colors that are adjacent to each other in the circle constitute, in fact, a harmonious color scheme.

Complementary Colors

The colors that are in opposing positions in the above-mentioned circle are called complementary colors. They are: yellow and purple, red and green, blue and orange. There is always only one color complementary to another. In painting, when the two colors of each pair are mixed together, a neutral grey results. When colored lights that are each other's complements are mixed, white light will result. Complementary colors are opposites, they balance each other out. Complementary colors mutually reinforce each other when they are placed next to each other, but they destroy each other when they are mixed together and form grey.

Cold and Warm Colors

The colors of the spectrum can be divided into cold and warm colors. In the color circle the warm zone begins with yellow and ends with purple; the cold colors are located in the other half. Each of the two groups has a totally different character. Colors with a warm character are expressive, exciting, and very conspicuous. Cold colors are much more modest and subtle. They have a relaxing effect but, if not enough contrasts are used, a garden designed with cold colors may seem boring.

Warm colors have a higher degree of brightness. In comparison to cold colors they are lighter. A light-colored object seems larger than a dark-colored object, hence an object with a warm color seems larger as well. This makes it seem closer, while the dark, cold colors tend to seem more distant. You can make your garden seem larger by taking advantage of this effect. Use cold colors in the back of the garden so the end of the garden seems farther away and gives a suggestion of depth.

The purple of the *Erigeron* "Nachthimmel" contrasts strongly with the yellow of the common yarrow because purple and yellow are complementary colors.

In this graph, all the color squares of the same brightness are located on one horizontal line. Orange and green have the same degree of brightness and so do red and blue. Yellow is highest in the graph; it is the brightest color. Purple has the lowest degree of brightness. In order to give yellow the same degree of brightness as purple, it must be darkened with black. This creates an unsaturated yellow.

Top right
Colors are always influenced by surrounding colors. The orange lily-of-the-Incas is rather bright and conspicuous in comparison to the darker red of the rose.

Bottom right
The same lily-of-the-Incas is much darker next to the light yellow of the common yarrow and it therefore seems less bright.

The Three Dimensions of Color

Colors have three dimensions: tone, brightness, and saturation. These are important concepts that will be referred to regularly in this book.

Tone simply refers to the color, for example, red or yellow. A pure color does not contain white or black, nor does it contain other pigments. Pure colors hardly ever occur in nature, where colors always contain a second pigment or are influenced by the other color dimensions.

Brightness refers to how light or dark a color is. There are various gradations when approaching white as well as black. Four degrees of brightness have been indicated in the large color circle. In addition, the spectral colors have different degrees of brightness. The colors in the center of the spectrum (yellow to yellow-green) have a high degree of brightness; toward the two sides the brightness diminishes. Thus, pure yellow has a higher degree of brightness and is much lighter than pure purple. *Saturation* indicates how much black a color contains. The pure colors of the spectrum are intense and have a high degree of saturation. If black is added and mixed in, they become duller, and are called unsaturated.

The three dimensions are not isolated factors; rather they are influenced by the type of color. For example, when placed next to light yellow, orange seems darker and thus less bright. Next to red, orange looks lighter and, therefore, seems brighter. The two photographs of the lily-of-the-Incas show this clearly.

A Color Circle for Plants

The three dimensions of color can only be represented well in a three-dimensional double cone. Since, in a book, we are tied to the two dimensions of paper, color circles are generally used. The color circle that is represented here is a simplified version of the color cards of the Royal Horticultural Society (RHS). These color cards are used to determine the correct color of flowers and leaves.

Consider the color impression given by a flower. A white flower with a very small red-purple disk is white, but a white flower with rather large red-purple specks is classified as red-purple. Some flowers, such as phloxes or larkspurs, have two colors that run into each other. In these cases as well, the selection is made on the basis of the dominant color, i.e., the color that is most prominent when seen from a distance. This is also the important color when you use the plant in a specific color combination. The plant can now be assigned its number so that color combinations can be made also during the time when the plant is not blooming. For the tables in this book, the color groups between two colors, such as violet-blue between the colors violet and blue, for example, have been divided into two halves. The half on the side of violet has been classified as violet and the half on the side of blue as blue.

It is very useful for the gardener to be able to determine the exact color, but always take into account the subtle character of living colors. The process of determining a color has its limitations no matter how carefully it is done. The living color of a flower always shows some variation, changes frequently during the season, and is influenced by the adjacent colors in the garden and the angle of the light.

In the case of flowers that have either two colors or a darker disk, such as the summer phlox *Phlox maculata* "Omega" here, the dominant color is the one that is used to determine the color of the flower.

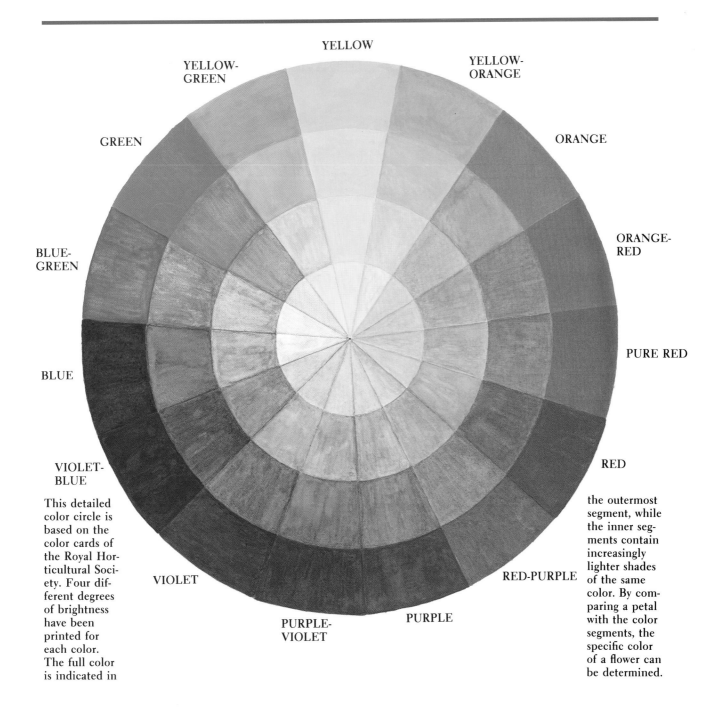

YELLOW

YELLOW-GREEN

YELLOW-ORANGE

GREEN

ORANGE

BLUE-GREEN

ORANGE-RED

BLUE

PURE RED

VIOLET-BLUE

RED

VIOLET

RED-PURPLE

PURPLE-VIOLET

PURPLE

This detailed color circle is based on the color cards of the Royal Horticultural Society. Four different degrees of brightness have been printed for each color. The full color is indicated in the outermost segment, while the inner segments contain increasingly lighter shades of the same color. By comparing a petal with the color segments, the specific color of a flower can be determined.

Colors and Their Names

The basic colors used are yellow, orange, red, purple, violet, blue, and green. In between there are the following colors: yellow-orange, orange-red, red-purple, purple-violet, violet-blue, blue-green, and green-yellow. Additionally, there are "greyed" colors; these are colors with low saturation. Brown, grey, black, and white are in this group as well. These colors have not been included in the circle. The RHS system of classifying colors has been generally accepted for use in the world of plants. Since it is important in a book about color to clearly indicate what particular color is being discussed,

this system has been adopted for use throughout the book.

On the other hand, this classification says nothing about the emotional value of colors. To express these, we have many names that suggest certain associations for colors, such as apple green, cherry red, honey-colored, or concepts such as mauve, pink, and lilac that add something personal to the name of a color. However, since these names may differ from person to person and depend on certain fashions, they make it hard to communicate precisely. This is the reason for a standard classification.

Left
A strong cold-warm contrast is provided by the cool blue-green of the ornamental grass *Agropyron pubiflorum* together with the warm orange-red of the *Salvia coccinea*.

Right
The light red-purple tulip is particularly conspicuous due to the light-dark contrast. Because there is only one light tulip while there are several dark ones, the light tulip catches the attention (quantity contrast).

Eight Color Contrasts

Our senses always perceive particular objects in comparison with other objects. Compared to low shrubbery, a 10-year-old birch tree is rather tall; however, next to a 150-year-old oak tree, that birch is just a small tree. Colors are also (unconsciously) compared with each other because the perception of a color is influenced by the color of the surroundings. The influences colors exert on each other can be divided into different contrasts. It is important to realize that, generally, different contrasts are present at the same time. In addition, the effect depends on the tone, or color, and also on the brightness and the saturation of the color.

When combining colors in a garden, it is handy to know something more about these different contrasts. They can be utilized to obtain special effects in the border, while undesired effects can be avoided.

Contrasts of Color Against Color
To obtain a simple contrast, use pure colors since all the pure colors contrast strongly when placed next to each other. The primary colors red, yellow, and blue provide the greatest contrast. Strong contrasts are also obtained by colors that are far removed from each other in the color circle. A good example is the combination yellow and purple, which produces a very beautiful, strong contrast in the garden if soft yellow is used. As the colors get further away from the three primary

colors, the contrasts decrease. Red-orange next to purple-violet contrasts less than red next to green.

Light-Dark Contrast
White and black together provide the greatest light-dark contrast, but this type of contrast can also be obtained with colors. Yellow is the lightest color and violet the darkest. The important element here is the brightness of the colors; starting out at yellow in the color circle, it decreases in both directions. In order to obtain a harmonious color combination, use proportionately less of a bright color than of a dark one. According to Itten, the harmonious proportion of yellow to purple, for example, is 1:3. The light-dark contrast also exists within borders of one color, for example, light purple flowers next to dark purple ones.

Cold-Warm Contrast
Cold and warm colors next to each other provide a strong contrast. Blue-green is the coldest color and orange-red the warmest. Whether a color gives the impression of being warm or cold also depends on the surrounding colors! The characteristics of cold colors are that they have a relaxing effect and seem thin, far away, and light. These qualities contrast with the characteristics of excitement, materiality, and heaviness of the warm colors.

29

Complementary Contrast

Two complementary colors next to each other reinforce each other, i.e., the colors seem brighter than when they are adjacent to any arbitrary other color. For example, yellow looks brighter next to purple than next to orange. But, in addition to the complementary contrast, other contrasts play a role. Yellow together with purple is also the strongest light-dark contrast, while orange together with blue provides a strong warm-cold contrast. Red and green have the same degree of brightness; here the complementary contrast is the main element. A good example from the garden is a red rose bush, where the red of the flowers contrasts beautifully with the green leaves. On the stems, the green and red sometimes tend to mix, thus creating interesting greyish colors.

Simultaneous Contrast

Our eyes always look for balance with regard to colors. This means that when we look at a color, our eyes will "ask" for the complementary color, that is, the "opposite" color. When that color is not present, our eyes will try to create it. When two color surfaces are placed next to each other, one color will dominate and force the other toward its complementary color. For example, grey leaves among orange flowers seem to be bluer as a result of the simultaneous contrast. Here, the extra blue

is evoked by the orange surface. Colors that are already each other's complements will seem brighter due to this effect. Gertrude Jekyll used the simultaneous contrast in garden designs by giving her single-color borders a seam of plants in the complementary color. The effect is that the color in the border seems brighter.

Successive Contrast

This contrast is related to the simultaneous contrast, but an element of time is involved. Here, the complementary color appears to the eyes only after some time, i.e., a colorful afterimage appears. This phenomenon can be easily tested by looking at and concentrating for a few seconds on a small colored surface, for example, yellow, and looking immediately afterwards at plain white paper. For a moment, an image will appear that has the same format but a complementary color, purple in this

Light yellow and violet are colors that contrast strongly with each other due to the light-dark contrast and also because they are almost complementary colors.

The grey of the two small grey circles in the center is exactly the same color. Due to the simultaneous contrast, however, the grey in the orange circle seems more blue.

case. Afterimages occur all the time in our visual perception, but we are generally not aware of them.

When making combinations, this afterimage is important. The color that is located a short distance away from the yellow surface is also slightly tinged by the purple afterimage. Blue flowers seem more purple when they are placed behind yellow ones than when they occur in isolation. Due to the fact that the purple is not really there but is instead only called up by our eyes, this contrast has an exciting, elusive effect. Gertrude Jekyll discovered that after looking at orange African marigolds for a long time the leaves seemed bluer. She used the phenomenon of successive contrast to prepare the eye for the color that would follow. Visitors to a garden in one specific color are led past flowers in the complementary color before they can look into the garden.

Quality Contrast

For this contrast, the saturation of colors is at issue. A bright, saturated color such as pure red contrasts with a dull, more cloudy color such as soft blue. The bigger the difference in saturation, the more of a distance there seems to be between the two colors. A bright red tulip above a haze of soft blue forget-me-nots really stands out and attracts extra attention, while the blue seems farther away. Hence one can obtain an obvious color accent by setting off a bright, saturated color against an area with a less saturated color.

Quantity Contrast

When very little of a color is used, that color will be particularly conspicuous. When there is one red flower in the middle of a white border, the red flower will be very conspicuous; if it is located among other red flowers, it will not be conspicuous. This effect can be used to make borders in a specific color more expressive by inserting flowers of a somewhat contrasting color in a few random spots in order to make the border more

conspicuous. In this case as well, the surroundings play an important part. A light yellow flower in a white border will not be as conspicuous as a red one. You will have to use a whole bouquet of the yellow flowers in order to obtain the desired effect!

Combining Colors Creatively

All the theoretical data discussed so far can be applied when faced with the most difficult part of gardening with colors, namely, combining the colors. Several specific color schemes have been developed for combining colors. They are used in various industries, such as interior decorating and textile weaving. However, if we assume that a garden can also be a work of art, individual creativity is to be preferred over prepared schemes. Theories can be studied, but information should be applied in unique and intuitive ways.

A satisfactory result will not be obtained in one year; it will generally take several years of experimenting. According to the painter Josef Albers, combining colors is like preparing a good meal, i.e., one should taste frequently. By being consciously involved with colors, we develop our feel for colors, and that is the important point.

Color Schemes

I want to present a simple classification of combinations here. There are basically two kinds of color schemes, harmonious and contrasting.

Colors that are harmonious with each other are related, i.e., they contain the same pigment. With the help of the color circle, simple, harmonious color combinations can be composed. A number of colors next to each other in the circle will always be harmonious, as long as the area is not too large. Red-purple, purple, and purple-violet, for example, go together very well, as do blue-green, green, and yellow. However, if colors of the same brightness are used, such a color scheme can sometimes be a little boring.

Contrasts make the entire picture more exciting and this aspect is discussed in the chapters on the various colors. Contrasts demand attention. Use them to accentuate a specific part of the garden that deserves attention. Remember contrasts are always dependent on the three dimensions of color: the tone of the color, the brightness, and the saturation. In addition, it cannot be pointed out often enough that all effects depend on the surrounding colors and light.

There are a number of color schemes that consist of various colors.

A very simple one is the *monochrome* color scheme, which consists of just one color. Variation can be obtained with different degrees of brightness of the color.

In every garden, green is of course present as the basic color. So it is really a matter of two colors. Only a green garden is truly monochromatic.

An *analogue* color scheme consists of a number of colors adjacent to each other in the color circle. This is a harmonious color scheme.

Then there is the contrasting *complementary* color scheme that consists of two complementary colors. Somewhat more complicated is a *double complementary* color scheme. For this, two colors that are adjacent in the circle are used together with their complementary colors. An example would be blue-green and blue together with red-orange and orange. However, this color scheme can also produce some very ugly results!

Still other color schemes can be obtained from the color circle, but they are often too polychromatic for a garden.

By arranging a bouquet in a specific color combination, you can judge if the colors go well with each other and are perhaps suitable for a border based on color.

Color is only the semblance of a thing that received its color from the light. Colorless is the light. No eyes can see it. Color does not constitute the essence of things
Herko Groot

Combining Plants

In order to determine beforehand whether a color combination will be successful, make a bouquet in the desired colors. If you use the same plants you want in your garden, you will obtain a reasonably good idea of the overall look. It is fun and informative to experiment with colors this way, and if the combination is disappointing nothing is lost. A picture of the prospective border can also be made with watercolors or colored pencils.

Always try to attain a certain balance when combining colors. This does not mean that there should not be quirks, but they must have some relationship to the color scheme as well. Balance is attained by selecting a theme. This may be one of shapes, but even in that case color plays a role. Unity is created by having the same color return again and again in the garden. If a particular part of the garden has to be differentiated from the rest, you can purposely interrupt the theme.

A quiet image can be obtained by placing plants with grey leaves among the colorful flowers. Grey-green is a neutral color that serves to connect the colors with each other. When two rather large areas of color, such as yellow and purple, are placed next to each other, they provide a more restful sight to the eyes if a little purple is used in the yellow and some yellow in the purple. In this case, it would be good, for example, to select purple flowers with yellow disks and to place a few purple flowers among the yellow ones.

Keep in mind that the color combinations in gardens are often seen from a distance. Cold colors are less conspicuous from a distance. Hence a subtle combination of different blues becomes less interesting at a distance. On the other hand, cold colors can be used to suggest depth in a garden by placing them in the back.

When many small flowers of different colors are planted close together the colors may become mixed when seen from a distance, just like the dots in a pointillist painting. This is sometimes beautiful, but the effect can also be dull and greyish.

In addition to the colors, the requirements of the plants must be taken into account as well. You cannot plan on having a plant that requires dry, rocky ground next to a marsh plant. In the paragraph about the selection of plants on page 41, you can read about all the things that must be kept in mind.

A GARDEN BASED ON COLOR

The color of a garden is the first thing we notice. Our senses register first of all its color and only then its shape and other elements. The colors used are therefore important for the first impression. But colors are important elements in determining atmosphere also when we look at greater length, because they influence our moods.

The Design

Producing a good design for a garden is not all that simple. The following cursory division of activities can be used as a working method. First, make a blueprint and measure everything carefully. Next, determine where there is shade and where full sun. Finally, list the desired parts so they can then be inserted on the blueprint. Now the complete design can be determined and a list of the plants compiled. The last element is, of course, the placement of the plants. However, with this sequence, there is no guarantee that a good design will be produced. Designing a garden is a lot of fun, but if you feel you are not up to it, don't hesitate to hire a landscape gardener. A good basis is extremely important, while details and plantings can always be adapted later on.

Part of the basis is the hard materials, such as the pavement, fences, and pergolas. These contribute to the total picture of the garden. There is a large selection of hard materials, also with regard to the color. Pleasing results can be obtained by making these colors agree (or contrast) with the plants. The colors of the house, walls, and window frames should also be taken into account. A white rambler, for example, does not show up very well against a white wall. A red or red-purple flower will produce much more effect.

In a book about color, it is not possible to deal with all aspects of design nor with elements such as layout and maintenance. Consult a good reference book about gardens when doing the layout for a garden.

Color in the Border

Most plantings based on color are in the form of borders. A traditional border is a rather narrow strip of plants that is closed off in the back by a wall or a hedge cut in straight lines and that runs along a lawn in the front. Many variations on this theme can of course be devised. The separation can also consist of isolated

Right
Hard materials also contribute to color combinations. In Monet's garden at Giverny the red-purple rose "Queen Elizabeth" contrasts beautifully with the framework for climbing plants that has been painted blue-green.

Far right, top
A colorful border, closed off in the back by an old wall overgrown with plants.

Far right, bottom
For this beautiful double border, only white-flowering plants have been selected. In order to make the whole image even more subtle, a few plants with grey-green leaves have been added.

shrubs or a fence. The border can be a raised strip; it can be adjacent to pavement; or it can be placed, like an island, in the middle of the lawn. And, because every layout of plants is different, every border will be different as well. Borders are generally laid out with lower plants up front and gradually taller plants toward the back, so all plants can be seen clearly. However, you can also select to have plants that are of the same height throughout. You can use cultivated plants with large colorful flowers or plants with small flowers that look very natural. Plants with large shapes can be alternated with finely shaped leaves and flowers. The groupings in the border can be large and clearly separated from each other or they can be mixed, which looks much more natural. The result depends totally on you, that is, on your personality, your feeling for color, your preference for specific plants, how you group the plants, and how you maintain it all.

Eight Steps for a Layout of Plants Based on Color

It is handy to follow a series of organized steps in designing a layout of plants based on color. To plant an entire garden, divide it into several related parts. Do the layout separately for each since this makes the work easier. In a larger garden, separate parts of the garden can each have a different color scheme.

Step 1
Determine which color(s) you want to use for the design. Get ideas from other gardens, books, and by experimenting with colors, for example in bouquets. The color circle and the theory presented in this chapter will be very helpful as well.

Step 2
Make a blueprint to scale of the garden or part of it. It is important that the measurements be accurate so the blueprint can later be filled in correctly.

Step 3
Determine how much light the plants will get. This information will be important when selecting plants later on. If the area receives at least seven hours of sunlight per day in the summer, it is considered fully exposed to the sun. With three to seven hours of full or filtered sunlight, it is considered half in the shade. With less than three hours full sun, it is considered a shady area. Determine also the kind of soil the garden has, and take it into account when selecting the plants. With these data, choose suitable plants from the tables in this book.

Step 4
Determine when most of the plants should flower (see the tables). If, for example, you go on vacation every July, you don't need many plants that bloom then. You can have one peak, but two main flowering periods are also possible. You might start in spring with a white-yellow combination followed in the summer by plants that have red-purple and purple flowers. This way, you can enjoy two different color schemes.

Colors are linked to the character of the seasons. Yellow and white are typical spring colors, being somewhat cool but light and bright. In the summer, colors are generally much more expressive and warmer. The fall has many warm colors as well, such as yellow, red, and the many shades of golden yellow; but there are also the colors of dying plants, such as brown and dark violet. The winter is very introverted, passive, and characterized by cold colors.

Step 5
Make a list of plants that are suitable for your design. The points to keep in mind when making a selection are discussed in the next section of this chapter. The tables also list the number of plants per square yard.

Step 6
The plants must now be spaced out over the area available. With the help of the information on your list of plants, make a layout. Try to create a balanced whole, as far as both color and shape are concerned. Take into account the effect the colors will have on each other. And consider another important point: How will the entire garden look without flowers? Flowers will only bloom for a few weeks, so be sure the plants will look attractive during the rest of the year as well!

Step 7
Fill in everything on the blueprint. To get an idea of the effect, color in the drawing with colored pencils or paint. Then check once more that everything fits together well. Keep the blueprint for later use; you can use it to record how the results look and to make any possible adjustments. The report will be complete if you also keep a garden diary. There you can make notes every summer about mistakes you made and new plants you have seen somewhere else. A garden is never finished. . . .

Step 8
Start the planting in the fall or spring.

The first step in making a border based on color is the selection of the colors.

The Garden

The wide border: the fine rich colors of columbine, lupine and larkspur

Here the sun shines with a quieter and deeper light

The bees hum, and there is the fragrance of jasmine.

P.N. van Eyck

When selecting the plants, pay attention to shapes as well. In this combination, a beautiful contrast of shapes is provided by the round flowers of the rose "Raubritter" and the long, thin spikes of *Salvia* × *superba* "East Friesland."

Selecting the Plants

I find it is handy to give some structure to the large group of garden plants by dividing the plants into groupings. For the garden, choose among shrubs (subdivided in trees and bushes), perennials, annuals, biennials, bulbs, and tubers. Among the plants in a border, all the different types may be represented, although trees will not often be included and perennials will be the main ingredient.

When making a list of plants, there are a number of things to be considered. Most of the information about these can be found in the tables at the end of the chapters on the individual colors.

The first item, of course, is *color*, both the color of the flowers and the leaves. It is not always easy to determine exactly what color the flowers of a plant will have. In descriptions in lists and books, subjective wording is often used to indicate the colors; even photographs can misrepresent colors. If it turns out later that you have estimated certain colors incorrectly and they do not fit into the overall picture, the plants will have to be replaced. It is, of course, safest to first determine the colors of the plants yourself, aided by the color circle. If the plants you selected are in this book, get the correct colors from the tables.

When you want to combine colors, it is important to know the *flowering times*. It would be a shame to miss out on that beautiful color combination because one of the plants flowers in April and the other in June!

Shape is also important when making a selection. Make sure there is some variation by combining, for example, flat umbelliferous plants and plants that have slim spikes or by using graminaceous leaves next to the almost round leaves of a *Hosta*. Beautiful leaves are also important because plants flower only a short period of the year.

The *height* and *width* of a plant are important elements to be considered in the selection of the right location for the various plants. Tall plants are generally placed toward the back, but they can also rise up from among a bed of low plants. In the tables you will find the average height of the plants.

Finally, consider the needs of the plants themselves. If a plant is placed in a spot where it does not feel happy, it will not do well and it will get sick more easily, thus giving little pleasure. Therefore, take into account the plant's *need for light* as well as its *soil requirements*.

WHITE

Left
This romantic white bench fits in beautifully among the white flowers and the grey-green leaves. Here the white variety of the wisteria stands on a graceful trunk.

White has always been the symbol of all that is good, all that is pure. It stands for innocence, virginity, simplicity, and in many cultures it is the color of brides. At weddings, white flowers are symbols of hope, love, and happiness. White carnations and white roses are traditional in the West. In Asia, jasmine, the symbol of friendship, is displayed at weddings. In Western art as well, white flowers are the symbol for purity and innocence. In the art of the Renaissance, the white Madonna lily (*Lilium candidum*) or the white rose represents the Virgin Mary, while the red rose represents the blood of Christ. To the Romans, the white lily was the symbol of modesty, royalty, and perfection, and it was dedicated to the goddess Juno.

On the other hand, white does have a negative connotation because it is the color of winter and the color of death. White flowers, such as white roses and calla lilies, are also displayed at funerals. In Islam, the white *Iris albicans* is planted on graves as the flower of death, and in China white is the color of mourning.

The expression "Whatever is too white becomes dirty quickly" means that too great a friendship is no good. White also has a negative meaning in war. A white flag is used to indicate surrender.

In color therapy, a preference for white denotes a conservative outlook.

Top
The jasmine *Philadelphus lemoinei* "Belle Etoile" flowering exuberantly in May and June.

THE WHITE GARDEN

The most well known garden in white is the white garden of Vita Sackville-West in Sissinghurst. White flowers are shown to full advantage especially in the evening and on beautiful summer nights because they reflect all the available light. In 1949, Vita conceived the idea of making a white garden precisely because she was fond of strolling through the garden in the evening. It is a splendid garden and tens of thousands of people visit it every year. The flower beds, enclosed by low hedges with straight lines, consist of many different plants with grey leaves, such as *Artemisia* and plants with white flowers, of course. There are roses, *Clematis*, phloxes, calla lilies, and many more beautiful flowers.

A garden with only white-flowering plants is attractive because of the simplicity it projects. A white garden also has a subtle, relaxing effect and has a somewhat mysterious effect in the dark. The splendid concealed garden of Greys Court in England is, in fact, extra mysterious because of the exclusive use of white-flowering plants.

It is rather easy to make a list of plants for a white garden since it is hard to go wrong with the color. Choose from hundreds of plants, because there is a white-flowering variety of almost every garden plant. The words *alba*, *album*, or *albus* often appear in the name. In the table at the end of the chapter is a selection of suitable plants for the white garden.

You cannot create a white garden simply by using white flowers only. It is the mix of white with grey-green and green leaves that makes the garden exciting. Try to obtain a balance between white and green by distributing the plants well. Structure is imparted to the garden as a whole by regularly repeating the same white. Since there is not much color, the contrasts in shape between leaves and flowers are of great importance. Pay special attention to shapes when selecting the plants.

Even white comes in different shades. Our eyes can detect the smallest differences in shading! And usually at least a little color is to be seen in white flowers, certainly in the disk. For example, the petals of the white-flowering *Geranium clarkei* "Kashmir White" have very fine red-purple veins and the *Lychnis chalcedonica* "Alba" is actually a very light orange.

In order to keep the white garden from becoming monotonous, use different shades of white. When the color of the disk is the dominant color, red-purple for example, as in the case of some small carnations, the flower can no longer be categorized as white but belongs with the red-purple flowers.

Grey-green leaves are indispensable in a white garden. Combined with dark green leaves, white appears

I love color, which I truly enjoy, but white is glorious forever.

Vita Sackville-West

African Garden (excerpt)

The thin blue shines through the tall hedges that greenly surround this little valley full of light; here, white flowers sway their little faces as they deliberate their silent secret.

W. Hessels

The famous white garden of Sissinghurst Castle, in England, designed by Vita Sackville-West.

Top left
A corner in Vita's white garden with white foxglove, *Gillenia trifoliata*, grey-leaved cotton thistle, and several varieties of *Artemisia*. Under the beautiful pear *Pyrus salicifolia* stands Tomas Rosandic's mysterious statue "Virgin."

Bottom left
Among Ton ter Linden's gardens is this admirable white garden. The Latin name of the white mullein is *Verbascum chaixii* "Album."

Top right
Grey-green leaves are indispensable in a white garden. Here, the white foxglove is combined beautifully with the sturdy cotton thistle (*Onopordum*).

Bottom right
Obvious accents in this white garden are provided by the green-and-white-variegated leaves of the dogwood *Cornus alba* "Elegantissima" and the dark leaves of the smoke tree *Cotinus coggygria* "Krumhout."

harsh and may be too glaring due to the light-dark contrast. Grey leaves make white seem softer and they link the groups of white flowers with each other.

COMBINATIONS WITH WHITE

White is a neutral color that fits in with everything. In the following chapters on each color, you will read more about white as a color to be combined with the other colors.

In a colorful border, white can provide the necessary restfulness and separate the colors from each other. Create combinations with white and the colors will be made more lively because of the white. This happens especially for colors with a low degree of brightness, such as purple and blue. On the other hand, next to the brightness of white, colors seem darker and may lose some of their expressiveness.

White is greatly influenced by adjacent colors. Next to dark green leaves, white roses seem to have a very light red color. The complementary color of green (red) is projected, so to speak, onto the white flowers so that the roses will appear to be light red (simultaneous contrast). This same effect occurs of course also with other colors.

White is not a color, as has been explained in the introduction to this book. A white surface reflects almost all light rays and is the "color" with the greatest brightness. Hence white stands out especially in a shady corner or in the evening. In fact, flowers that are pollinated by moths always have light colors. As an extra attraction, they often have a delightful fragrance. A good example is the annual ornamental tobacco plant (*Nicotiana*).

White in Plant Names

albiflors—with white flowers
albomarginata—white-edged
albus (-a, -um)—white
argenteus—silvery white
candicans—whitish
candidum—bright white
dealbata—white
lactiflora—with milk-white flowers
leucanthemum—with white flowers

WHITE IN
LEAVES AND
TRUNKS

White combined with green often occurs in leaves as well. Green-and-white-variegated leaves can be used to great advantage in a white garden and they are also perfect for combinations with other colors. The word *variegata* often occurs in the scientific name for green-and-white-variegated plants. The variegated day lilies, such as *Hosta crispula* and *Hosta fortunei* "Marginato-alba," are very well known examples. The mint, *Menta rotundifolia* "Variegata," has both green-and-white-variegated leaves and a fragrance. Also very suitable are the green-and-white-variegated ornamental grasses, such as the *Holcus mollis* "Albovariegatus." A beautiful shrub with green-and-white-variegated leaves that has been used in the design for the white garden is the dogwood, *Cornus alba* "Elegantissima." The Japanese angelica, *Aralia elata* "Variegata," with its green-and-white-variegated leaves, has a beautiful shape and does not grow very tall. Plants with green-and-white-variegated leaves are in the White Table.

A well-known tree with white bark is, of course, the birch. The trunk is most beautiful in the *Betula costata*, the *B. utilis* "Jacquemontii," and the *B. papyrifera*. There are also plants with white berries that can be used in a white garden. These include Doll's-eyes or *Actaea pachypoda*, snowberries *Symphoricarpos*, which grow in a somewhat untidy manner, and certain kinds of rowan berries, such as the *Sorbus* "Red Tip."

Top left
White foxglove
and bellflower
do not need
much light.

Top right
Green-and-
white-varie-
gated Japanese
angelica *Aralia
elata* "Varie-
gata."

Right
Light orange
flowers of the
rambler "René
André" among
green-and-
white-varie-
gated leaves of
Cornus alba
"Elegan-
tissima."

Left
Green-and-
white-varie-
gated leaves of
this *Hosta* pro-
vide a strong
accent with
shape as the
important ele-
ment.

49

A GARDEN IN WHITE

In this romantic white garden with a tightly laid-out format, a great selection of white-flowering plants has been used together with plants that have grey leaves since these combine so well with the white flowers. The tight layout provided by hedges gives the garden adequate structure and contrasts beautifully with the plants that grow in rather exuberant profusion. In time, the *Taxus* hedge provides a dense separation so you can sit undisturbed on the terrace. Trim the hedge from the very beginning, so it will be wider at the bottom than at the top. Leave some space between the hedge and the other plants. This will allow the hedge to get sufficient light throughout, so it fills out well. The same applies for the much lower *Buxus* hedges.

In the back of the garden, a simple pergola will be erected to provide support for several climbers. You can also use a fence of individual poles. The pavement can be made with small red or yellow bricks; cemented cobblestones or tiles are also suitable. In the center of the pavement an area has been blocked out where there is a racemose stem of white roses, and this serves as the focal point of the garden. Sufficient room remains to make a nice area for sitting.

The design can be adjusted to the shape of your garden. If you want to make the garden longer, enlarge the terrace or extend the borders more. If the garden is much narrower, the "island" in the pavement can be left out.

In the border, flowering begins in March with the windflower *Anemone blanda* "White Splendour." Also very nice are the snowdrops, which flower even earlier. Flowering continues until October, with the white roses and Japanese anemones. In the back of the garden on the right is the willow-leaved pear, which is the most beautiful grey tree in existence; on the left is the dogwood with green-and-white-variegated leaves. In addition, a number of small shrubs have been used and many perennials. In short, this is a garden you can enjoy the year round.

1 Dusty miller, *Lychnis coronaria* "Alba"

2 Life everlasting, *Anaphalis triplinervis*

3 Ornamental onion, *Allium nigrum*

4 *Artemisia absinthium* "Lambrook Silver"

5 Lupine, *Lupinus* "Noble Maiden"

6 Columbine, *Aquilegia* "Silver Queen"

7 Ornamental tobacco, *Nicotiana sylvestris* + *Tulipa* (Viridflora tulip) "Spring Green"

8 Windflower, *Anemone blanda* "White Splendour"

9 Wormwood, *Artemisia ludoviciana* "Silver Queen"

10 Butterfly bush, *Buddleia davidii* "White Profusion"

11 Summer phlox, *Phlox decussata* "Pax"

12 Grey-green couch grass, *Agropyron pubiflorum*

13 Regal lily, *Lilium regale*

14 Whitewood, *Aster divaricatus*

15 Variegated dogwood, *Cornus alba* "Elegantissima"

16 Chinese wisteria, *Wisteria sinensis* "Alba"

17 Japanese anemone, *Anemone hybrida* "Honorine Jobert"

18 Virgin's-bower, *Clematis* "Huldine"

19 *Rosa* "Maria Mathilda"

20 *Crambe cordifolia*

21 Rambler, *Rosa* "Climbing Snow Queen"

22 Masterwort, *Astrantia major* "Margery Fish"

23 Virgin's-bower, *Clematis* "Madame Lecoultre"

24 Weeping willow-leaved pear, *Pyrus salicifolia* "Pendula"

25 Virgin's-bower, *Clematis montana*

26 *Viburnum burkwoodii*

27 Larkspur, *Delphinium* (Pacific Giant-hybr.) "Galahad"

28 Loosestrife, *Lysimachia ephemerum*

29 Bellflower, *Deutzia x rosea* "Campanulata"

30 Peach-bells, *Campanula persicifolia* "Alba"

31 Love-in-a-mist, *Nigella damascena* "Alba"

32 *Rosa*, "Snow Queen"

33 Dwarf English boxwood, *Buxus sempervirens* "Suffruticosa"

34 English yew, *Taxus baccata*

The grey-leaved plants can be found in the Green Table.

DESIGN AND LIST OF PLANTS

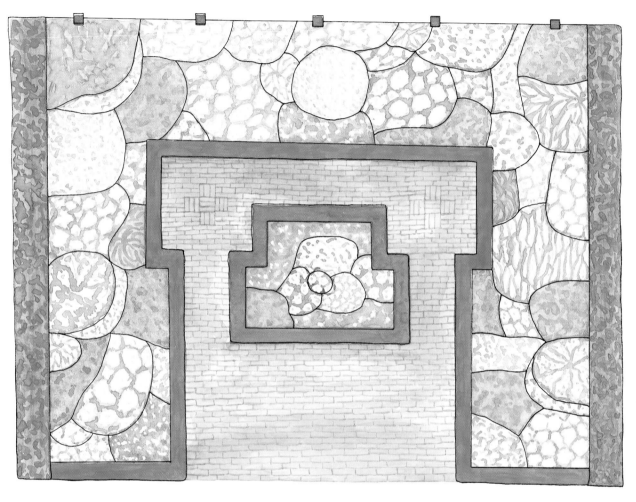

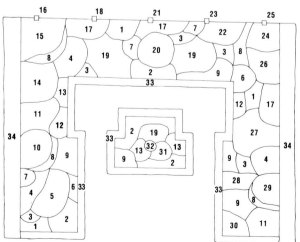

Design: Modeste Herwig. Measurements: 26 × 21½ ft. (8 × 6.5 m.)

WHITE TABLE

NAME	COMMON NAME	BLOOM/ MONTHS	LIGHT	HEIGHT IN INCHES	TYPE	PLANTS PER YD^2	NOTES
Achillea macrophylla	Milfoil	6–8	○ ◐	50–60	○	3	creamy white
Achillea ptarmica plena "The Pearl"	Sneezewort	7–8	○ ◐	20–30	○	5	wilted plant
Acidanthera bicolor var. murilae	Hardy gladiolus	7–8	○	20–30	⊛	9	not winter hardy
Actaea pachypoda	White baneberry	5–8	◐ ◑	8–12	○	5	white berries, damp soil
Agastache foeniculum "Album"	Anise hyssop	7–8	○ ◐	20–40	○	7	bee plant
Allium nigrum	Flowering onion	5–6	○	30–40	⊚	12–16	too tender for many areas
Ammi majus	Bishop's weed	6–10	○	20–30	⊙	9–11	good cut flower
Anemone blanda "White Splendour"	Wind flower	3–4	○ ◐	3–4	⊛	12–16	soak before planting; eaten by rodents
Anemone hybrida "Honorine Jobert"	Japanese anemone	9–10	○ ◐	24–30	○	5–7	hardy perennial
Anthericum liliago	St. Bernard's lily	6–7	○	20–30	○	9	good cut flower
Aquilegia "Silver Queen"	Columbine	5–6	○ ◐	20–30	○	9	
Aralia elata "Variegata"	Japanese angelica	8–9	◐	25–30 ft	⊕ ✦		variegated leaves
Aster divaricatus	White wood aster	9–10	○	20–30	○	7	
Aster pringlei "Monte Cassino"		9–10	○	20–30	○	7	
Astilbe arendsii "Snowdrift"	False spiraea	7–8	○ ◐	10–20	○	7	
Astrantia major "Margery Fish"	Great masterwort	6–8	○ ◐	20–30	○	7	green and white
Buddleia davidii "White Profusion"	Butterfly bush	7–9	○	to 10 ft	⊕		prune back in spring
Campanula carpatica "White Clips"	Bellflower	6–8	○ ◐	4–10	○	7–9	
Campanula lactiflora "White Pouffe"	Bellflower	6–8	○ ◐	12	○	7	
Campanula latifolia "Alba"	Bellflower	6–7	○ ◐	30–40	○	5–7	
Campanula persicifolia "Alba"	Peach-bells	6–7	○ ◐	20–30	○	7	
Centaurea montana "Alba"	Mountain bluet	5–8	○ ◐	10–20	○	5–7	
Cerastium biebersteinii	Chickweed	5–6	○	4–12	○	5–7	grey-green leaves
Chrysanthemum frutescens	Marguerite	5–10	○	10–40	⊕	5–7	not winter hardy
Chrysanthemum leucanthemum	Oxeye daisy	6–9	○	12–24	○	7	
Cimicifuga racemosa "Atropurpurea"	Snakeroot	9–10	○ ◐	40–50	○	5–7	grey-purple leaves
Cimicifuga simplex "The Pearl"	White pearl	9–10	○ ◐	30–40	○	5	
Clematis "Huldine"	Virgin's bower	7–9	○ ◐	to 10 ft	⊕	1	climber
Clematis "Madame Le Coultre"	Virgin's bower	6–9	○ ◐	to 10 ft	⊕	1	climber
Clematis montana	Anemone clematis	4–5	○ ◐	to 26 ft	⊕	1	climber
Clematis recta	Virgin's bower	7–8	○ ◐	40–60	○	1	wilted plant
Cornus alba "Elegantissima"	Tartarian dogwood	5–6	○ ◐	to 15 ft	⊕	1	variegated leaves
Cosmos bipinnatus "Purity"		5–10	○	40–50	⊙	2–3	
Crambe cordifolia	Colewort	7–8	○	to 7 ft	○	1	
Delphinium "Ivory Towers"	Larkspur	6–8	○	60–70	○	5–7	creamy white
Delphinium pacific giant "Galahad"	Larkspur	6–7	○	70–100	○	5	
Deutzia × rosea "Campanulata"	Slender deutzia	4–5	○ ◐	40–50	⊕	1	
Dianthus plumarius "Artis"	Grass plumerius	5–6	○	4–6	○	9	grey-green leaves
Dicentra formosa "Alba"	Western bleeding-heart	5–9	◐	6–18	○	7–9	grey-green leaves
Dictamnus albus "Albiflorus"	Gas plant	6–7	○	30–40	○	5	flowers exude combustible gas
Digitalis purpurea "Alba"	Common foxglove	6–7	○ ◐ ◑	40–80	○ ⊙	7	
Echinacea purpurea "White Lustre"	Coneflower	6–8	○	40–80	○	7	butterfly plant
Epimedium grandiflorum	Barrenwort	4–5	◐	6–10	○	9–11	foliage plant, ground cover
Eremurus himalaicus	Desert candle	5–7	○	60–80	○	2–3	well-drained soil
Erigeron karvinskianus	Fleabane	5–9	○	8–12	○	7–9	turns red-purple as it wilts
Eupatorium rugosum	White snakeroot	7–10	○ ◐	50–60	○	3	fluffy inflorescence
Exochorda racemosa	Pearlbush	4–6	○ ◐	to 10 ft	⊕		
Filipendula purpurea "Alba"	Meadowsweet	7–8	○ ◐	20–40	○	5	damp soil
Galtonia candicans	Summer hyacinth	6–9	○	30–40	⊚	5–7	not winter hardy
Gaura lindheimeri "Whirling Butterflies"		7–9	○	30–40	○	7	sensitive to frost
Geranium clarkei "Kashmir White"		5–7	○ ◐	8–16	○	7	
Gillenia trifoliata	Bowman's-root	6–8	○	30–50	○	3	
Gypsophila paniculata	Baby's-breath	6–8	○	30–40	○	3–5	short-lived in hot, humid climates
Hesperis matronalis "Alba"	Sweet rocket	5–8	○ ◐	30–50	⊙	5	butterfly plant
Holcus mollis "Albovariegatus"		6–7	○	20–30	⊙	3–5	striped ornamental grass
Hosta crispula	Hosta	7	○ ◐ ◑	10	○	5	leaves have white margins
Hosta fortunei "Marginato-alba"	Hosta	7	○ ◐ ◑	8–16	○	5	leaves have white margins
Hosta plantaginea "Grandiflora"	Hosta	8–9	○ ◐	20	○	7	large white flowers

NAME	COMMON NAME	BLOOM/ MONTHS	LIGHT	HEIGHT IN INCHES	TYPE	PLANTS PER YD²	NOTES
Hosta sieboldiana "Elegans"	Hosta	6-7	○◐●	20-30	perennial	1-2	blue-green leaves
Houttuynia cordata		6-7	○◐	6-8	perennial	7	leaves have grey-purple spots
Hyacinthoides hispanica "Alba"	Spanish bluebell	4-6	○◐	8-12	bulb	12-15	spreading plant
Hydrangea paniculata "Tardiva"	Panicle hydrangea	7-9	○◐	to 25 ft	shrub	1	prune back in spring
Hydrangea petiolaris	Climbing hydrangea	6-7	○◐●	to 60 ft	shrub	1	climber
Iberis sempervirens "Snowflake"	Edging candytuft	4-6	○	4-10	shrub	7-9	evergreen
Iris sibirica "White Swirl"	Siberian iris	5-6	○◐	30-40	perennial	7	dependable, long-lived perennial
Lamium maculatum "White Nancy"	Spotted dead nettle	5-7	◐●	6-10	perennial	7-9	grey-green leaves
Lavandula angustifolia "Alba"	English lavender	5-7	○	10-20	shrub	5-7	grey-green leaves
Lavatera trimestris "Mont Blanc"	Tree mallow	5-10	○	30-50	annual	5-7	very showy flowers
Lilium "Sterling Star"	Lily	7-8	○◐	30-50	bulb	9-11	with small, dark specks
Lilium candidum	Madonna lily	6-7	○	30-40	bulb	9-11	
Lilium regale	Regal lily	7	○	30-50	bulb	9-11	white with burgundy red
Linaria purpurea "Alba"	Toadflax	5-9	○	30-40	perennial	7	
Lupinus "Noble Maiden"	Lupine	6-7	○◐	30-50	perennial	3	difficult in hot-summer area
Lychnis coronaria "Alba"	Campion	6-8	○◐	20-30	perennial biennial	5-7	grey-green leaves
Lysimachia ephemerum	Loosestrife	6-8	○	20-40	perennial	5-7	grey-green leaves
Magnolia stellata	Star magnolia	3-4	○◐●	to 25 ft	shrub		flowers tend to be frost-resistant
Malus "Gorgeous"	Crabapple	4-6	○	to 25 ft	shrub tree		small red apples
Malus "John Downie"	Crabapple	5	○	to 25 ft	tree		small red-orange apples
Malva moschata "Alba"	Musk malva	6-8	○◐	20-40	perennial	5	
Mentha rotundifolia "Variegata"	Horsemint	6	○◐	20-30	perennial	5-7	invasive; variegated leaves
Monarda "Snow White"	Bee balm	7-9	○◐	30-50	perennial	7	mildew can be a problem
Narcissus triandus "Thalia"	Angel's tears	4-5	○◐	18-24	bulb	15-20	not eaten by rodents
Nectaroscordum siculum		5-6	○◐	30-40	bulb	12-15	red-purple disk
Nicotiana sanderae "White Bedder"	Flowering tobacco	6-10	○◐	20-30	annual	9-11	
Nicotiana sylvestris	Flowering tobacco	7-9	○◐	60-70	perennial	5-7	
Nigella "Miss Jekyll Alba"	Love-in-a-mist	6-9	○	10-20	annual	7	
Paeonia lactiflora "Duchesse de Nemours"	Peony	5-6	○	30-40	perennial	3	with many petals
Philadelphus "Dame Blanche"	Mock orange	5-6	○	to 7 ft	shrub		fragrant
Phlox carolina (suffruticosa) "Miss Lingard"	Thick-leaf phlox	6-8	○◐	40-50	perennial	9	
Phlox paniculata "Pax"	Summer phlox	7-9	○◐	50-60	perennial	5-7	
Physostegia virginiana "Summer Snow"	Obedience	7-9	○	30-40	perennial	7	
Polygonum amplexicaule "Album"	Smartweed	7-9	○	40-50	perennial	3	
Pulmonaria saccharata "Sissinghurst White"	Lungwort	4-5	◐●	10	perennial	7-9	leaves with white spots
Pyrus salicifolia "Pendula"	Willow-leaved pear	4-5	○	to 10 ft	shrub		leaves with white spots
Rodgersia pinnata "Alba"		7-8	◐	30-40	perennial	5	foliage plant
Rosa "Intergant (Elegant Pearl)"	Miniature rose	6-8	○	10-20	shrub	3-5	
Rosa "Maria Mathilda"	Polyanthus rose	6-10	○	30-50	shrub	3	
Rosa "Mme Plantier"	Rose	6-7	○	60-80	shrub	1	
Rosa "Sally Holmes"	Rose	6-9	○	to 7 ft	shrub	1	
Rosa "Snow Queen"	Polyanthus rose	6-10	○	30-50	shrub	3	
Rosa "Winchester Cathedral"	Rose	6-9	○	to 7 ft	shrub	1	fragrant
Salvia coccinea "White"	Mealy-cup sage	6-10	○	20-30	perennial	7-9	cultivated as an annual
Scabiosa caucasica "Perfecta Alba"	Pincushion flower	7-9	○◐	30-40	perennial	5-7	
Selinum tenuifolium		7-10	○	30-50	perennial	5	flat-topped inflorescence
Sidalcea candida		6-9	○	24-32	perennial	7	flowers again in late summer
Smilacina racemosa	False spikenard	5-6	◐●	20-30	perennial	7	
Spiraea × vanhouttei	Bridal-wreath	5-6	○	to 10 ft	shrub	1	
Thalictrum aquilegifolium "Album"	Meadow rue	5-7	○◐	30-40	perennial	5-7	
Thalictrum delavayi "Album"	Meadow rue	7-8	○◐	60-70	perennial	5	
Tiarella cordifolia	Foamflower	5-6	◐●	4-8	perennial	7-9	ground cover
Tulipa viridiflora "Spring Green"	Tulip	5	○	20	bulb	15-20	white with green stripes
Verbascum chaixii "Album"	Mullein	7-8	○	30-50	perennial	5	
Verbena hastata "Alba"	Blue vervain	7-9	○	30-40	perennial	7	
Veronica virginica "Alba"	Culver's root	7-8	○	50-70	perennial	5	
Viburnum burkwoodii		3-4	○◐	to 7 ft	shrub	1	fragrant
Viburnum opulus	Cranberry bush	5-6	○◐●	to 13 ft	shrub		red berries
Viola cornuta "Milkmaid"	Horned violet	6-10	○◐	4-8	perennial	9-11	
Wisteria sinensis "Alba"	Chinese wisteria	4-5	○◐	to 33 ft	shrub	1	climber

○ full sun; ◐ partial shade; ● shade

O perennial plant; ⊙ biennial; ○ annual; bulb; tuber; shrub; tree

YELLOW

Yellow is a bright, happy color. Yellow is the color of the sun and, like orange and red, it is a warm and stimulating color. Although red is a much warmer color, yellow reminds us of the warm rays of the sun that make the budding yellow-green leaves appear in the spring, as well as many yellow flowers such as daffodils, crocuses, *Forsythia*, primroses, lesser celandines, and spring sunflowers.

As the brightest color, yellow is symbolically linked to knowledge and the ability to think. In paintings of the Old Masters, yellow (or gold, the noble metal) was the symbol of the hereafter or the heavenly light. Saints were depicted with a halo of bright yellow around their heads. In the Far East, yellow is the color of wisdom and, in fact, is a holy color in Buddhism. In Tenth Century China, yellow was reserved exclusively for the imperial court. Pure yellow is light, but it immediately loses its brightness and becomes unattractive when mixed with even a very small quantity of another color. Cloudy yellow represents untruth, falsehood, and doubt. In contrast to the meaning it had in Asia, yellow was considered a sign of enmity or treason in Europe as early as the Middle Ages. Yellow was linked to Judas and the victims of the Spanish Inquisition. Traditionally, yellow is the color of hatred and envy. This ensues from the tradition that bile is responsible for feelings of envy and resentment. A well-known expression that developed from this idea, "to spew his bile," means to express one's ire, outrage, or malice. In the psychological color therapies, someone with a preference for yellow is considered a creative, inventive person with a passion for life who can, however, be combative and aggressive as well. Yellow stimulates the brian and nerves and has, characteristically, a harmonizing effect.

THE YELLOW GARDEN

As Gertrude Jekyll said, a "golden" garden looks very sunny. If you like yellow, a golden garden is perhaps the thing for you. Yellow is a real eye-catcher, it stands out without being obtrusive. This is why it is also very suitable for a small corner that deserves extra attention.

In addition to yellow-flowering plants, many plants with yellow-green leaves (see the Green Table) and plants with yellow-and-green-patterned leaves (see the Yellow Table) can be used. And there are, of course, many different shades of yellow, such as green-yellow, light yellow, vivid yellow, orange-yellow. Light yellow is often called lemon yellow or sulphur yellow, and creamy white is really a very light shade of yellow. These different kinds of yellow provide sufficient variation in the yellow garden. Just as in a white garden or other one-color garden, contrasts of shape are very important in the yellow garden as well.

Yellow looks extra bright next to dark colors; for example, in front of a dark *Taxus* hedge, next to the dark green leaves of a *Hosta*, or in a shady little corner where the yellow almost seems to light up. The green of the surrounding leaves has a favorable effect on yellow. As Johannes Itten put it, "Since green is a mixture of yellow and blue, yellow acts as if it is visiting an acquaintance." Dark, purplish leaves (for example, those of the smoke tree) can provide a nice accent, while a small amount of white conveys something refreshing to the entire image. In the Yellow Table, you will find an ample choice of plants with yellow flowers as well as plants with yellow-and-green-variegated leaves.

Yellow
shines the
light of the
lamp in the
night
Yellow is the
autumn with
its seasoned
glory
Yellow is the
flower in the
grassy lawn
Yellow is the
color of tak-
ing action to
go on
Herko Groot

To enter sud-
denly into
the Golden
Garden, even
on the som-
berest day,
is like com-
ing into the
light of the
sun.
Gertrude Jekyll

Left
A yellow border with just a few orange accents. Large groups of goldenrod (*Solidago*) afford lots of color.

Right
The beautiful shrub rose "Maigold" in a walled garden.

Left [1]
The soft yellow-white-grey border in the Model Gardens, including yellow *Phlomis samia,* dark-leaved fennel, grey lamb's ears, and the dark-leaved smoke tree "Royal Purple."

Left [2]
The soft yellow-green of the lady's-mantle recurs in the disk of the *Iris sibirica* "Fourfold White."

Right
A combination in soft yellow, yellow-green, and bright red produced by soft yellow *Phlomis samia,* Lupine "Chandelier," tall giant scabious, Lady's-mantle, and red *Geum chiloense* "Mrs. Bradshaw."

Left [3]
Yellow common yarrow and yellow-and-red columbine make a beautiful combination.

Left [4]
A combination of grey-leaved *Artemisia ludoviciana* "Silver Queen," yellow common yarrow, and yellow-green lady's-mantle.

COMBINATIONS WITH YELLOW

Bright yellow is a difficult color to use in combinations. It can, of course, be used very well in the yellow garden, but soft yellow is generally much better for combinations.

Very refreshing is the combination of yellow and white. Next to white, yellow seems darker and, hence, less shiny. In such a combination it is fine to use bright yellow; for example, white summer phloxes, white larkspurs, daisies, common yarrow, tickseed, and evening primroses. Bright yellow is most conspicuous on a black background, but that will not often happen in a garden.

Very beautiful with soft yellow are white, grey, and dark leaves. In Lunteren, Rob Herwig has laid out a wide border in these colors; the border design for this chapter has been adapted from that border. The dark, grey-purple leaves (purple with some black mixed in) cause the yellow to appear brighter and the grey leaves link all the colors with each other.

A very exciting combination is yellow, green-yellow, and bright red. Yellow acquires an extra strong shiny glow next to the warm red. Only very little red needs to be used because it stands out considerably next to yellow. In addition, red shows up well due to the quantity contrast created: for example, red roses, yellow-green ornamental tobacco, lady's mantle, and yellow common yarrow.

Read more about yellow with orange and red in the next chapter. Yellow with red-purple (pink) is discussed in the chapter "Red-Purple." Yellow with its complementary color purple or with blue is found in the chapter "Color Contrasts."

Yellow in Plant Names

auratum—with golden yellow specks
aureomarginata—with golden yellow edges
aureus (-a, -um)—golden yellow
citrinus—lemon yellow
flavum—light yellow
lutens—yellow
melanochrysum—dark golden
semperaurea—always golden yellow
vitellinum—egg yellow

Left
Yellow-white-grey border with dark accents in the Model Gardens.

Bottom left
The miniature rose "Intergant" among seedlings of the fennel "Giant Bronze."

Right
Leaves of the ornamental grass *Carex firma* "Variegata" combine well with goldenrod *Solidago* "Goldkind."

Bottom
Foxglove *Digitalis ferruginea* among blades of the ornamental grass *Deschampsia cespitosa.*

GREEN-AND-YELLOW VARIEGATED LEAVES

In yellow gardens, yellow-and-green-variegated leaves are also very beautiful. The holly *Ilex aquifolium* "Golden van Tol" has a golden yellow edge along its leaves. The golden-yellow-and-green-variegated meadow foxtail *Alopecurus pratensis* "Aureovariegatus" has a yellow edge along the long blades of grass. The ornamental grass *Carex* "morrowii Aurea-Variegata" grows rather tall and has a very narrow yellow edge along its leaves. The wintry green leaves of the Japanese laurel (*Aucuba*) have yellow specks. Many different varieties of ivy have yellow-and-green-variegated leaves, such as the *Hedera colchica* "Sulphur Heart," with large yellow-and-green-variegated leaves, and the *Hedera helix* "Goldheart," which has small leaves with a yellow disk.

61

In the fall, there is of course an abundance of yellow leaves. Leaves that fade into a gorgeous yellow in the fall are those of witch hazel, serviceberry, birches, various maples, day lilies, and all kinds of ornamental grasses. In the winter, when all the leaves have disappeared, the dogwood *Cornus stolonifera* "Flaviramea" will still show its yellow branches.

BORDER IN YELLOW, WHITE, AND GREY WITH DARK LEAVES AS ACCENTS

This is a border in a soft color combination, that looks extremely natural. These plants create picturesque effects especially at the beginning or end of the day when the angle of the light is particularly beautiful. To get an idea of the effects, look at the photograph of the white mini rose among the seedlings of the fennel. The soft yellow combines fantastically well with the dark leaves of the smoke tree and the dark plantain. As time goes by, the plants will of course become more intermingled as they grow and new combinations will continue to appear. This definitely applies to fennel and plantain, whose seeds spread enormously! They are therefore plants that should be watched. If you want to add other annual plants, red orach (*Atriplex hortensis* "Red Plume") would be very suitable. This is a plant whose seeds spread considerably; you will have new plants every year. The various kinds of ornamental tobacco are beautiful and include white *Nicotiana sanderae* "White Bedder" and *N. sylvestris*, and yellowish green *N. sanderae* "Limegreen" and *N. langsdorffii*. A beautiful soft yellow is the annual California poppy *Eschscholzia caespitosa* "Sundew" with very fine, grey-green leaves.

The plants have been grouped in such a way that this border can be viewed from two sides. On one side could be a path and on the other a lawn. In the center of the border stands a dark-leaf maple, which can grow rather tall. In the original border are also two old oak trees. Hence, the plants can manage with a certain amount of shade.

The design is by Rob Herwig. You can see it with real plants at the Model gardens, where this border was planted a few years ago.

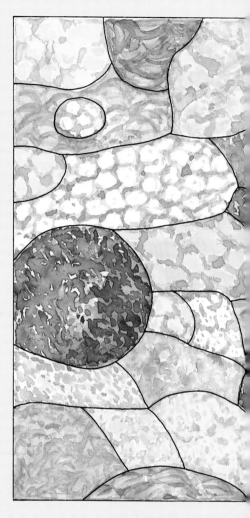

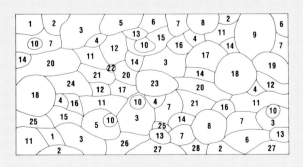

Design: Rob Herwig. Measurements: 26 × 13 ft. (8 × 4 m.)

The dark-leaved plants can be found in the Purple Table.

DESIGN AND LIST OF PLANTS

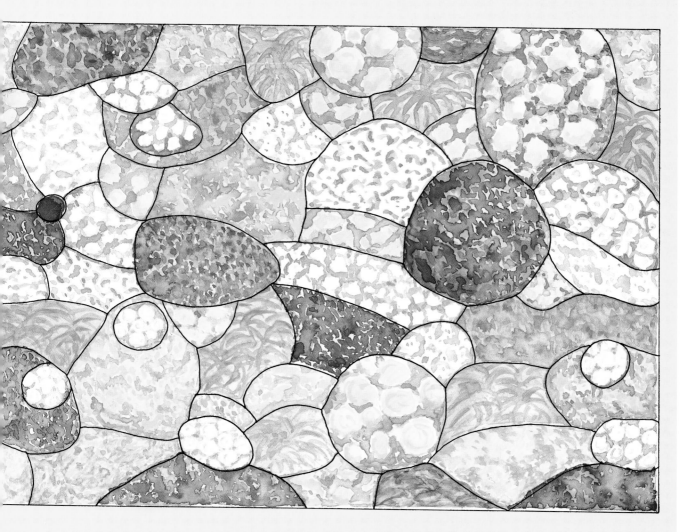

1. Columbine, *Aquilegia chrysantha*

2 Plantain, *Plantago major* "Purpurea"

3 Lady's-mantle, *Alchemilla mollis*

4 Fritillary, *Fritillaria pallidiflora*

5 Alumroot, *Heuchera micrantha* "Palace Purple"

6 Cypress spurge, *Euphorbia cyparissias*

7 Grey-green couch grass, *Agropyron pubiflorum*

8 *Rosa* "Dorothé"

9 Bronze fennel, *Foeniculum vulgare* "Giant Bronze"

10 *Rosa* "Snow Queen"

11 Artemisia, *Artemisia absinthium* "Lambrook Silver"

12 Obedience, *Physostegia virginiana* "Javelin"

13 Miniature rose, *Rosa* "Intergant" ("Elegant Pearl")

14 Yellow foxglove, *Digitalis grandiflora*

15 Life everlasting, *Anaphalis triplinervis*

16 Lily, *Lilium* "Sterling Star"

17 Bellflower, *Campanula latifolia* "Alba"

18 Smoke tree, *Cotinus coggygria* "Royal Purple"

19 Cosmos, *Cosmos bipinnatus* "Purity"

20 Japanese anemone, *Anemone hybrida* "Honorine Jobert"

21 Black snakeroot, *Cimicifuga ramosa* "Atropurpurea"

22 Norway maple, *Acer platanoides* "Crimson King"

23 *Houttuynia cordata*

24 Lupine, *Lupinus* "Chandelier"

25 Ornamental tobacco, *Nicotiana langsdorffii*

26 Yellow archangel, *Lamiastrum galeobdolon* "Herman's Pride"

27 Four-leaf clover, *Trifolium repens* "Pentaphyllum"

28 *Platystemon californicus*

YELLOW TABLE

NAME	COMMON NAME	BLOOM/ MONTHS	LIGHT	HEIGHT IN INCHES	TYPE	PLANTS PER YD²	NOTES
Achillea "Moonshine"	Yarrow	6–8	○	20–30	○	5–7	light yellow
Achillea "Schwefelblüte"	Yarrow	6–8	○	20–30	○	5–7	light yellow
Achillea filipendulina "Parker's Variety"	Fern-leaf yarrow	7–8	○	40–60	○	5	
Achillea millefolium "Hoffnung"	Common yarrow	6–8	○ ◐	30–40	○	7	light yellow
Achillea millefolium "Martina"	Common yarrow	6–8	○ ◐	30–40	○	7	light yellow
Achillea taygetea	Yarrow	7–9	○ ◐		○	7	light yellow
Aconitum lamarckii	Monkshood	6–8	○ ◐	20–30	○	9	light yellow
Aconitum septentrionale "Ivorine"	Wolfsbane	7–8	○ ◐	30–40	○	9	light yellow
Alchemilla mollis	Lady's-mantle	6–8	○ ◐	10–20	○	7	yellow-green
Allium moly	Flowering onion	6–7	○	10–20	⚘	12–16	
Alopecurus pratensis "Aureovariegatus"	Meadow foxtail	5–6	○	30–50	○	5	leaves have yellow stripes
Anthemis "E.C. Buxton"	Chamomile	7–9	○	30–50	○	5	light yellow
Aquilegia chrysantha "Yellow Queen"	Columbine	6–8	○ ◐	40–50	○	9	light yellow
Asphodeline lutea	King's-spear	5–6	○	40–50	○	2–3	sensitive to frost
Aucuba japonica "Variegata"	Lily of the valley	3–4	○ ◐	to 10 ft	♣	1	yellow spotted leaves
Bupleurum falcatum	Hare's-ear	7–9	○ ◐	30–40	○	5	
Carex elata "Aurea"	Sedge	5–7	○ ◐	30–50	○	3	leaves have yellow stripes
Cephalaria gigantea	Scabiosa	7–8	○	6–9 ft	○	3	light yellow
Clematis tangutica	Virgin's bower	6	○ ◐	to 10 ft	♣	1	climber
Convallaria majalis "Aureo-variegata"	Lily of the valley	5	◐ ● ▓	6–10	○	7–9	leaves have yellow stripes
Coreopsis grandiflora	Tickseed	7–8	○	20–30	○	7–9	
Coreopsis verticillata "Moonbeam"	Tickseed	6–9	○	10–20	○	7–9	light yellow
Cornus stolonifera "Flaviramea"	Yellow-twig dogwood	5–6	○ ◐	to 10 ft	♣	1	yellow branches
Corylopsis pauciflora	Buttercup winter hazel	3–4	○ ◐	72	♣	1	light yellow
Crocus chrysanthus "Cream Beauty"	Crocus	2–4	○ ◐	2–4	⚘	20–25	light yellow
Crocus flavus	Yellow crocus	3	○ ◐	2–4	⚘	20–25	
Cytisus praecox	Warminster broom	4–5	○	to 10 ft	♣	1	light yellow
Digitalis ferruginea	Rusty foxglove	7–8	○ ◐	60–70	○ ☉	7	yellow-orange with brown spots
Digitalis grandiflora	Yellow foxglove	6–8	◐	30–40	○ ☉	7	light yellow
Doronicum orientale	Leopard's bane	4–5	○ ◐ ▓	10–20	○	7	
Erythronium tuolumnense "Pagoda"	Trout lily	4	◐	10	⚘	7	light yellow
Eschscholzia caespitosa "Sundew"	California poppy	7–9	○	4–10	☉	9–11	grey-green leaves; light yellow
Foeniculum vulgare "Giant Bronze"	Fennel	7–8	○	50–60	○ ☉	5	grey-purple leaves
Forsythia intermedia	Forsythia	4	○ ◐	to 10 ft	♣		
Fothergilla major		4–5	○	to 10 ft	♣		autumn orange; light yellow flowers
Fritillaria pallidiflora	Fritillary	4	◐	12–16	⚘	7–9	light yellow
Hamamelis mollis	Chinese witch hazel	12–2	○ ◐	to 30 ft	♣		
Hedera colchica "Sulphur Heart"	Colchis ivy	8–10	○ ◐	to 16 ft	♣	1	climber; yellow spotted leaves
Hedera helix "Gold Heart"	English ivy	8–10	○ ◐ ▓	to 26 ft	♣	1	yellow spotted leaves
Helianthus decapetalus	Thin-leaf sunflower	8–10	○	40–60	○	5	
Heliopsis helianthoides	Oxeye	7–9	○	40–60	○	5	
Hemerocallis "Corky"	Daylily	6–8	○ ◐	40–50	○	3–5	
Hemerocallis "Green Flutter"	Daylily	6–8	○ ◐	40–50	○	3–5	yellow-green
Hemerocallis citrina	Daylily	6–8	○ ◐	40–50	○	3–5	
Hosta fortunei "Aurea"	Plaintain lily	7	○ ◐ ▓	20–30	○	5	yellow-green leaves
Ilex aquifolium "Golden van Tol"	English holly	5–6	○ ◐ ▓	to 33 ft	♣	1	leaves have yellow edges
Iris "Butter and Sugar"	Siberian iris	6	○ ◐	30–40	○	7	yellow with white
Kirengeshoma palmata		9–10	◐ ●	40–50	○	5	light yellow; beautiful leaves
Kniphofia "Little Maid"	Red hot poker	7–9	○	30–40	○	3–5	light yellow
Kniphofia citrina	Red hot poker	7–8	○	30–40	○	3–5	light yellow
Laburnum waterei	Golden-chain tree	5–6	○	to 25 ft	♣ ✤		
Lamiastrum galeobdolon "Herman's Pride"	Yellow archangel	5–7	◐ ●	12–24	○	7–9	beautiful patterned leaves
Ligularia dentata "Desdemona"		8–9	○ ◐	30–50	○	3	grey-purple leaves
Ligularia przewalskii		7–8	○ ◐	30–50	○	3	
Lilium "African Queen"	Lily	7–8	○ ◐	40–50	⚘	9–11	
Lilium "Golden Splendour"	Lily	7–8	○ ◐	40–50	⚘	9–11	light yellow
Lonicera periclymenum	Honeysuckle	6–9	○ ◐	to 13 ft	♣	1	climber; red berries
Lupinus "Chandelier"	Lupine	6–7	○ ◐	40–50	○	3	light yellow

NAME	COMMON NAME	BLOOM/ MONTHS	LIGHT	HEIGHT IN INCHES	TYPE	PLANTS PER YD²	NOTES
Lysimachia nummularia	Pennywort	5–7	○ ◑	2	○	7–9	ground cover
Meconopsis cambrica	Himalayan poppy	6–10	○ ◑ ▦	24	○	5–7	
Milium effusum "Aureum"	Millet grass	4–6	◑	50–60	○	5	yellow-green ornamental grass
Narcissus "February Gold"	Daffodil	3–4	○ ◑	6–10	bulb	15–20	
Narcissus "Hawera"	Angel's-tears	4–5	○ ◑	6–16	bulb	15–20	
Nepeta govaniana	Catmint	7–9	○ ◑	24–32	○	7	light yellow
Oenothera biennis	Evening primrose	7–9	○	10–70	biennial	5–7	
Oenothera tetragona "Yellow River"	Evening primrose	6–8	○ ◑	20–30	○	7	
Phlomis samia		6–7	○	30–40	○	3–5	light yellow
Platystemon californicus	Creamcups	6–8	○ ◑	12	biennial	12–15	light yellow
Potentilla "Yellow Queen"		6–8	○	10–20	○	7	
Primula veris	Cowslip	4–5	○ ◑	4–10	○	9	light yellow
Rhododendron molle "Adriaan Koster"	Azalea	5	○ ◑	to 7 ft	shrub	1	
Rodgersia podophylla "Braunlaub"		8	◑	50–60	○	5	light yellow; grey-orange leaves
Rosa "Dorothé"	Rose	6–10	○	30–50	shrub	3	light yellow
Rosa "Freedom"	Polyanthus rose	6–10	○	30–50	shrub	3	
Rosa "Golden Showers"	Climbing rose	6–9	○	to 10 ft	shrub	1	
Rosa (David Austin-roos) "Graham Thomas"	Rose	6–9	○	to 10 ft	shrub	1	fragrant
Salvia officinalis "Icterina"	Common sage	6–7	○	10–20	shrub	7	yellow spotted leaves
Scabiosa ochroleuca	Pincushion	7–11	○	20–30	○	5	light yellow
Sedum acre	Stonecrop	6–7	○ ◑	4–6	○	7–9	
Sedum telephium maximum	Orpine	8–9	○	16–24	○	7	grey-green/grey-purple leaves
Sisyrinchium striatum	Blue-eyed grass	6–7	○	20–30	○	7	light yellow; sensitive to frost
Solidaster hybridus "Lemore"		9	○	20–30	○	7	light yellow
Symphytum grandiflorum	Comfrey	4–5	◑ ▦	10–20	○	5–7	light yellow
Thalictrum flavum spp. *glaucum*	Meadow rue	6–7	○	60–80	○	3	light yellow
Trollius "Earliest of All"	Globe flower	5–6	○ ◑	20–30	○	7	light yellow
Tulipa fosteriana "Yellow Purissima"	Tulip	4	○	12–20	bulb	15–20	
Verbascum "Gainsborough"	Mullein	6–8	○	30–40	biennial	5	light yellow
Verbascum nigrum		6–8	○ ◑	30–40	○	5	
Viola cornuta "Gazelle"	Horned violet	6–10	○ ◑	10–20	○	9–11	light yellow
Viola cornuta "Irish Molly"	Violet	6–10	○ ◑	4–8	○	9–11	brown with yellow-orange

○ full sun; ◑ partial shade; ▦ shade
○ perennial plant; ⊙ biennial; ○ annual; ⊛ bulb; ⊕ tuber; ⊛ shrub; ⊛ tree

Left
In the yellow-red garden in Sissinghurst common yarrow flowers look especially beautiful against the dark green *Taxus.*

Right
A fresh combination of colors consisting of the white flowers of foxglove and the yellow ones of the leopard's-bane *Doronicum orientale.*

65

ORANGE

L ike yellow, orange is associated with the sun and with fire and warmth. Yellow is a borderline color between the warm and cold colors. When mixed with green, yellow immediately becomes somewhat cool. But orange is truly a warm, radiant color.

This notwithstanding, there are not very many associations for orange because it is viewed as a mixed color; it is neither red nor yellow. Until the Tenth or Eleventh Century, the word orange did not even exist in Dutch. It only came into existence when the orange became known in the Netherlands and the French name for the fruit, *l'orange*, was adopted. Later it became the color of the Dutch royal family.

Bright orange is a festive, lively color. It is also very conspicuous, especially in the case of fluorescent orange, which makes it appropriate for use as a warning color in traffic. A less saturated, dark orange tends towards brown and reminds us of the fall, when the leaves of the trees take on beautiful shades of orange. But even bright orange is associated with the fall and the many orange or orange-red berries that mature at that time of year.

In color therapy, orange has a soothing, positive, invigorating, and encouraging effect. Like yellow, it stimulates the nerves and is the color of warmth, willpower, and temporary authority.

Left
The leaves of the Japanese maple *Acer palmatum* in their marvellous autumn color.

Top
Bright orange flowers of the lily-of-the-Incas combined with grey-leaved artemisia.

THE ORANGE GARDEN

I would think that there are very few gardens with orange flowers only. Orange is such an expressive, dominant color it soon becomes too much. Use it very subtly: only a small amount in an area of green leaves and other colors with low saturation. Bright orange will then stand out even more next to the unsaturated colors, due to the quality contrast and, additionally, due to the quantity contrast. Orange is the perfect color for a surprise in a secluded corner of the garden. Toward evening especially, the effect is rich and warm.

Gertrude Jekyll designed an orange garden, but in addition to orange she used yellow and red as well. Since orange is situated between yellow and red, the use of these three colors is a perfect combination. Among the plants in her design were African marigolds, orange coneflowers, lilies, sneezeweed (*Helenium*), and red-hot pokers (*Kniphofia*). The orange garden was placed just before a grey garden, which produced the successive contrast. After all that orange, the grey looks much more beautiful because it seems bluer.

Light orange is very modest and easy to use in a garden. It is sometimes called apricot or salmon. Unfortunately, there are not very many flowers with this color. They are mostly annuals such as *Arctotis* "Apricot," the marigold *Calendula officinalis* "Apricot Beauty," the non-climbing nasturtium *Tropaeolum* "Orange Whirleybird," which grows to a height of 16 in. (40 cm), and the Cape marigold *Dimorphotheca sinuata*.

Less saturated brown shades will result when a little black is mixed in with orange. In this category are the beautiful orange colors of the fall and also the color of terra-cotta earthenware and bricks. A brick path fits in beautifully with an orange garden because the less saturated brown softens the orange of the flowers.

Potted Plants in Orange

Would you like to enjoy blazing orange without having a whole garden in this color? Then plant a terracotta pot with plants that have orange flowers. They look beautiful next to the natural orange-brown of the pot. The lily "Enchantment" could be a radiant focal point and, along the edges, the monkey flower *Mimulus* "Orange Glow." Perfect choices for softening the orange somewhat are the light orange annual Cape marigold (*Dimorphotheca*) and the horned violet "Chantreyland."

Left
An orange border with lily-of-the-Incas, light orange lilies, and many grey-green leaves of the *Artemisia ludoviciana* "Silver Queen."

Top right
The monkey flower (*Mimulus*) is generally cultivated as an annual in the Netherlands. Among all the green leaves, the orange flowers look beautiful here along the water's edge.

Center right
Light orange has a totally different character from intense orange. A combination with very tender colors is produced by light orange roses together with the variegated leaves of irises.

Bottom right
The color of the flowers of the *Begonia sutherlandii* is repeated in the less saturated orange color of the terra-cotta pot.

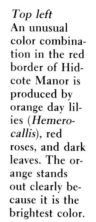

Top left
An unusual color combination in the red border of Hidcote Manor is produced by orange day lilies (*Hemerocallis*), red roses, and dark leaves. The orange stands out clearly because it is the brightest color.

Center left
The soft orange of the rose "English Garden" is set off well against the dark leaves of the red orach and the grey-green of the artemisia "Silver Queen."

Bottom left
A combination of warm colors consisting of soft yellow common yarrow (**Achillea taygetea**), orange monkey flowers, lily-of-the-Incas, and the red rose "Kolima."

Right
The light orange rambler "Talisman" grows here among the white-flowering virgin's-bower *Clematis montana*.

COMBINATIONS WITH ORANGE

As already shown by Miss Jekyll, yellow, orange, and pure red make a very successful combination because of the impression of warmth that is created. In the Model Gardens in Lunteren, the Netherlands, the large border has been planted in these colors. In order to make it a little more subtle, soft yellow was chosen. In front of the border is a wide lawn that produces a restful green foreground. The border design in this chapter is based on this sunny border.

White makes orange less expressive because the orange looks much darker next to white, which is extremely light. Light orange, on the other hand, goes well with white and creamy colors. Dark purplish leaves and grey-leaved plants are beautiful in this combination: for example, the light orange rose "English Garden" and grey artemisias (*Artemisia*); as well as the red orach and cream-colored *Echinacea purpurea* "White Lustre," which has an orange-brown disk.

Grey leaves reinforce orange, as can be seen in the photograph of the lily-of-the-Incas (*Alstroemeria*) with artemisias (*Artemisia*). Hard materials in grey shades can also be used to make orange stand out beautifully. Orange also combines very well with green, which is always present in the garden. The simultaneous contrast between green and orange makes orange seem more red and somewhat warmer. A less saturated orange (orange with a little black) produces brown and coppery colors. This can be seen in wallflowers (*Erysimum*), in sneezeweed (*Helenium*), and, of course, in leaves with beautiful fall colors. These warm colors combine well with soft yellow, bright orange, and purple or violet. A very well known example of orange leaves with purple flowers is a group of Michaelmas daisies in front of a shrub in colorful fall foliage. Terra-cotta or brick also combines beautifully with complementary shades such as violet-blue and blue.

In the chapter "Color Contrasts" are combinations of orange with purple, light orange with light violet, and orange with its complementary color, blue. The combination orange with red-purple is generally not considered pleasing, and it would be better to avoid this combination in the garden.

Orange and Brown in Plant Names

aurantiacus (-a, -um)—orange
cupreata—copper-colored
brunnea—brown
fuscus—dark brown
rubiginosa—with rust-brown hairs

ORANGE IN LEAVES, BERRIES, AND BARK

Most berries are orange or orange-red for a practical reason. Birds are particularly sensitive to this color and they are the ones who must spread the seeds that are present in the berries in order to ensure the continued existence of the species.

In the fall, combinations that are a blaze of color can be made with berries. European spindle trees (*Euonymus*) are already busy making their own combinations. Their brilliantly colored seeds are surrounded by a husk in a contrasting color. *E. europaeus* has orange seeds and red-purple fruit, a strange color combination!

The sea buckthorn (*Hippophae*) will grow in the poorest soil. This shrub grows on dunes and produces many edible but sour orange berries that make a beautiful color combination with its grey leaves. It is necessary to place a male and a female shrub next to each other, otherwise there will be no berries. The apples of the ornamental apple unfortunately are not edible but they are very beautiful. *Malus* "John Downie" is a nice variation with many apples that vary in color from yellow to orange-red.

A well-known plant is the fire thorn (*Pyracantha*), which is often made to grow up along the walls of buildings but which can also grow very well without support. Rose hips are not only edible for birds, but for people as well. The hips of the *Rosa moyesii* are a beautiful orange to orange-red. The orange-red hips of the brier rose (*Rosa canina*) are the most appropriate for making jam, but the hairy little seeds must be removed. The sweetbrier (*R. rubiginosa*) and the Japanese rose (*R. rugosa*) have beautiful hips. The berries of the rowan (*Sorbus*) come out as early as August. There are many beautiful varieties with fruits of different colors.

The last colors of the season are generally provided by leaves, not flowers. We can admire the blazing oranges and rust-browns of fall in maples (*Acer*), serviceberries (*Amelanchier*), various European spindle trees (*Euonymus*), *Fothergilla*, the oak trees *Quercus pontica* and *Q. rubra*, and the sumac (*Rhus*).

A more saturated orange is to be found throughout the year in the rather small, graceful maple *Acer griseum*. Its peeling bark, which is very conspicuous, has a beautiful orange-brown color. It is perfect as a solitary little tree in a small garden. Very unusual is the ornamental grass *Carex buchananii*, whose leaves remain grey-orange all summer; this is an orange with some black mixed in so it is less saturated.

In the autumn, the sumac *Rhus typhina* "Dissecta" begins very subtly to take on its fall colors.

BORDER IN YELLOW, ORANGE, AND RED

The border in yellow, orange, and red is based on the oldest border in the Model Gardens. The colors used are sometimes called men's colors. Orange and pure red especially are warm and expressive, and they have a somewhat "masculine" character. Gertrude Jekyll had already used orange together with yellow and red. This wide border shows once more that these colors make a fantastic combination. Intense yellow is not used; soft yellow, found in common yarrow, for example, is a much more subtle combination with the other two exuberant colors. The red should be pure red; if a more red-purple is used, it clashes badly with the other colors. In contrast with the conspicuously colored flowers, the surroundings have been kept rather quiet. In front of the border is a large lawn that provides a green foreground with straight lines. I recommend inserting an edge of hard material between the plants and the lawn to keep the grass from growing into the border. A brick wall made of open, grey bricks made from stone dust provides a quiet, neutral background against which the warm colors show up even better. The intensely red rambler "Parkdirektor Riggers" grows against the wall. If you do not want to put up a wall, a hedge will also make a perfect background. In that case, of course, do without the rambler.

A number of plants in this border need some extra protection during rainy winters; among these are the *Lobelia*, the Montebretia, and the lilies. The remainder of the plants are winter-hardy perennials and include red as well as soft-yellow roses. The high point of this sunny border comes in July, but the roses continue to flower and give it color from June until the first night frosts.

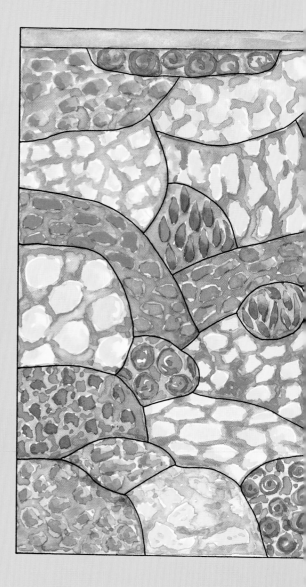

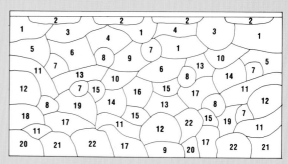

Design: Rob Herwig. Measurements: 26 × 13 ft. (8 × 4 m.)

DESIGN AND LIST OF PLANTS

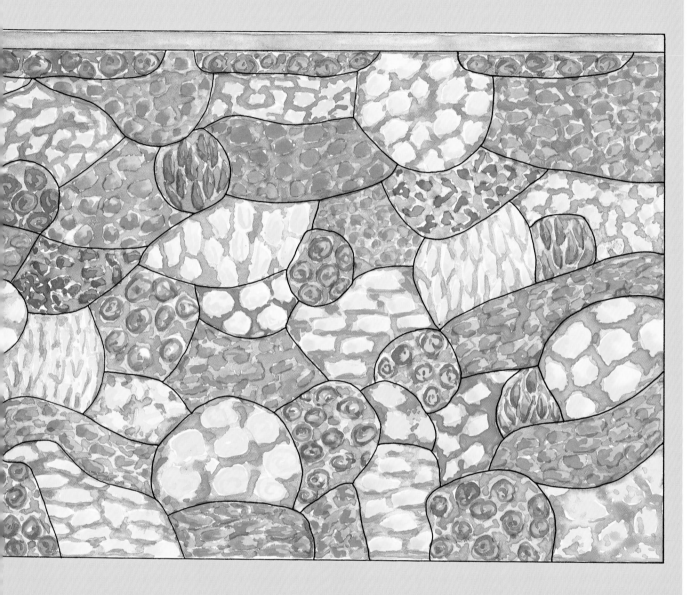

1 Lily-of-the-Incas, *Alstroemeria aurantiaca* "Orange King"

2 Rambler, *Rosa* "Parkdirektor Riggers"

3 Pincushion flower, *Cephalaria gigantea*

4 Yellow meadow rue, *Thalictrum flavum*

5 Yellow chamomile, *Anthemis hybrida* "E.C. Buxton"

6 Lupine, *Lupinus* "Chandelier"

7 Cardinal flower, *Lobelia cardinalis*

8 *Rosa* "Tojo"

9 Spurge, *Euphorbia griffithii* "Fireglow"

10 Montebretia, *Crocosmia* "Lucifer"

11 Trailing yallow, *A chillea tomantosum*, "King Henry"

12 Rose, *Rosa* "Dorothé"

13 Geum, *Geum* "Princess Juliana"

14 Red-hot poker, *Kniphofia* "Little Maid"

15 Trumpet lily, *Lilium* "Golden Splendour"

16 *Rosa* "Kolima" ("Lilli Marlene")

17 Common yarrow, *Achillea taygetea*

18 Geum, *Geum chiloense* "Mrs. Bradshaw"

19 *Phlomis samia*

20 Welsh poppy, *Meconopsis cambrica* "Aurantiaca"

21 Lady's-mantle, *Alchemilla mollis*

22 Miniature rose, *Rosa* "Zwergkönigin"

ORANGE TABLE

NAME	COMMON NAME	BLOOM/ MONTHS	LIGHT	HEIGHT IN INCHES	TYPE	PLANTS PER YD²	NOTES
Acer ginnala	Amur maple	4–5	○ ◐	to 20 ft	✳		orange autumn color
Acer griseum	Paperbark maple	4–5	○	20–40 ft	✳		grey-orange bark and autumn color
Achillea millefolium "Salmon Beauty"	Common yarrow	6–8	○ ◐	30–40	○	7	light orange
Alstroemeria aurantiaca "Orange King"	Lily-of-the-Incas	6–8	○	30–40	○	5–7	sensitive to frost
Amelanchier lamarckii		4–5	○ ◐	to 20 ft	✿ ✳		orange autumn color
Anthemis sancti-johannis	Chamomile	6–8	○	30–40	○	1	
Arumn italicum	Italian arum	4–5	◐ ●	6–12	○	7–9	orange fruit
Asclepias tuberosa	Indian paintbrush	7–9	○	30–40	○	7–9	
Begonia sutherlandii	Begonia	7–9	○	10–30	⊛	7	not winter hardy
Calendula officinalis	Pot marigold	6–10	○	20–30	☉	9	
Calendula officinalis "Apricot Beauty"		6–10	○	10–20	☉	9	light orange
Campsis radicans	Trumpet creeper	8–9	○	to 40 ft	✿	1–2	climber; sensitive to frost
Carex buchananii	Sedge	7	○ ◐	10–20	○	5–7	grey-orange leaves; ornamental grass
Chrysanthemum 'Duchess of Edinburgh"	Chrysanthemum	9–10	○	30–40	○	5–7	red-orange
Cosmos sulphureus "Diablo"	Yellow cosmos	7–10	○	to 7 ft	☉	3–5	
Crocosmia crocosmiiflora	Montbretia	7–9	○	30–50	⊛	5–7	sensitive to frost
Dimorphotheca sinuata "Salmon Queen"	Cape marigold	7–8	○	10–15	☉	7–9	light orange
Eremurus "Pinocchio"	Desert candle	6–7	○	40–60	○	5	well-drained soil
Erysimum allionii "Orange Queen"	Wallflower	4–5	○	10–20	☉	5–7	
Eschscholzia californica	California poppy	6–10	○	10–20	☉	9	
Euonymus europeaus	European spindle tree	5	○ ◐	to 20 ft	✿		orange fruit and autumn color
Euphorbia griffithii "Fireglow"		5–6	○ ◐	40–50	○	5–7	
Fothergilla major		4–5	○	to 10 ft	✿		orange autumn color
Fritillaria imperialis "Aurora"	Crown imperial	4–5	○	30–40	⬡	5–7	sensitive to frost
Geum "Princess Juliana"	Geum	5–7	○ ◐	20–30	○	7	
Glaucium corniculatum	Horned poppy	6–8	○	10–20	○	5	orange-red; grey-green leaves
Hamamelis intermedia "Jelena"	Witch hazel	1–2	○ ◐	to 13 ft	✿		
Helenium autumnale "Wyndley"		7–9	○	40–60	○	5–7	
Hemerocallis "Golden Prize"	Day lily	6–8	○ ◐	30–50	○	3–5	
Hemerocallis "Ruffled Apricot"	Day lily	6–8	○ ◐	30–50	○	3–5	light orange
Achillea tomentosum "King Henry"	Trailing yarrow	5–6	○ ◐	10–20	○	7	
Hippophae rhamnoides	Swallow thorn	3–4	○	to 30 ft	✿		orange berries; grey-green leaves
Kniphofia "Alcazar"		6–7	○	30–50	○	3–5	light orange
Kniphofia "Jonkheer van Tets"		8–9	○	30–50	○	3–5	
Lantana camara	Yellow sage	5–10	○	40–50	✿	7–9	cultivated as an annual
Ligularia dentata "Othello"		8–9	○ ◐	40–50	○	3	grey-purple leaves
Lilium "Enchantment"	Lily	7–8	○ ◐	30–50	⬡	9–11	
Lilium lancifolium	Tiger lily	8–9	◐	60–80	⬡	9–11	alkaline soil
Lonicera brownii	Honeysuckle	7–10	○ ◐	to 10 ft	✿	1	climber
Lychnis chalcedonica "Alba"	Maltese cross	6–8	○	48–56	○	7	light orange to white
Macleaya microcarpa "Kelway's Coral Plume"	Plum papaver	7–8	○ ◐ ●	to 10 ft	○	1	light orange; grey-green leaves
Meconopsis cambrica "Aurantiaca"	Welsh poppy	6–10	○ ◐ ●	16	○	5–7	
Mimulus "Orange Glow"		6–8	○ ◐	10–20	○	7	cultivated as an annual
Molinia arundinacea "Karl Foerster"		8–10	○	60–80	○	3	orange autumn color
Narcissus cyclamineus "Jetfire"	Daffodil	3–4	○ ◐	6–10	⬡	15–20	yellow and orange
Narcissus "Orangery"		4	○ ◐	6–16	⬡	15–20	white with orange corolla
Papaver orientale "Flamingo"	Oriental poppy	5–6	○ ◐	40–50	○	5	white with orange end
Papaver spicatum	Poppy	7–8	○	20–30	○	9	light orange
Phlox paniculata "Orange Perfection"	Summer bloom	7–9	○ ◐	50–60	○	5–7	
Physalis alkekengi var. *franchetii*	Chinese lantern	6	○ ◐	16–20	○	5–7	orange calyxes
Potentilla "William Rollisson"		6–8	○ ◐	12–20	○	7	yellow and orange
Primula aurantiaca	Primrose	7	◐	8–12	○	9	
Pyracantha coccinea	Fire thorn	5–6	○ ◐	to 10 ft	✿		orange berries
Quercus muehlenbergii	Chinkapin oak		○	to 18 ft	✳		orange autumn color
Rhododendron knaphill-exbury "Feuerwerk"	Azalea	5–6	○ ◐	to 7 ft	✿	1	
Rhododendron molle "Frans van der Bom"	Azalea	5	○ ◐	to 7 ft	✿	1	light orange
Rhus thyphina	Staghorn sumac	6	○ ◐	to 30 ft	✿ ✳		orange autumn color
Rosa "Just Joey"		6–10	○	30–50	✿	3	soft orange

NAME	COMMON NAME	BLOOM/ MONTHS	LIGHT	HEIGHT IN INCHES	TYPE	PLANTS PER YD²	NOTES
Rosa "Orangeade"	Polyanthus rose	6–10	○	30–50	shrub	3	
Rosa "Talisman"	Climbing rose	6–9	○	to 10 ft	shrub	1	light orange
Rosa "Westerland"	Climbing rose	6–8	○	to 10 ft	shrub	1	light orange
Rosa "English Garden"	Rose	6–9	○	to 8 ft	shrub	1	light orange; fragrant
Rosa moyesii	Rose	6	○	to 6 ft	shrub	1	red-orange hips
Rudbeckia fulgida "Goldsturm"	Coneflower	8–9	○	30–40	perennial	7	
Rudbeckia hirta	Black-eyed Susan	7–9	○	30–40	biennial	7	
Sorbus aucuparia	Rowan	5	○ ◐	to 60 ft	shrub tree		red-orange berries
Tagetes tenuifolia	Signet marigold	6–9	○ ◐	10–20	annual	7–9	small flowers
Trollius "Prichard's Giant"		5–6	○ ◐	20–30	perennial	7	
Tropaeolum "Orange Whirlybird"		7–10	○ ◐	8–12	annual	5–7	light orange
Tulipa "Apricot Beauty"	Tulip	4–5	○	8–12	bulb	15–20	light orange
Tulipa orphanidea "Flava"	Tulip	4	○	7–12	bulb	15–20	
Viola cornuta "Chantreyland"	Horned violet	6–10	○ ◐	4–8	perennial	9–11	light orange

○ full sun; ◐ partial shade; ◑ shade

◎ perennial plant; ⊙ biennial; ⊙ annual; ⊚ bulb; ⊛ tuber; ⊛ shrub; ⊕ tree

The yellow-orange-red border in the Model Gardens on which the border design in this chapter is based.

RED

Left
In the red border of Hidcote Manor, the bright red of the Oriental poppy is softened by the surrounding dark leaves.

The flaming red of the polyanthus "Tojo."

Red is a warm and vigorous color. It is the color of blood and, therefore, the color of life and death.

Red is a very important, "old" color. In practically every language, the naming of colors begins with black and white, while the first real color to be named is always red. It is the color that is noticed first and it is linked to strong, primitive emotions such as aggression, anger, joy, and lust. This dynamic, "masculine" color with a powerful radiance is associated with the (red) planet Mars and represents strength, war, passionate love, activity, and movement.

Orange-red especially is a stimulating, exciting color that increases blood pressure and accelerates respiration. It encourages aggression and is also associated with physical desire. Red also has a provoking effect on many animals, as in the case of a bull confronted with a red cloth.

Red is the color of the heart, which is always linked to love. A red heart indicates love. In India red is the holy color of the beautiful Lakshmi, the goddess of beauty and abundance.

Red is the color of the joy of living, but also of destruction and danger. A lot of blood is generally

not a good sign, and in traffic red stop lights and various red signs indicate danger. A hot-tempered person "sees red" or "turns red with anger."

In color therapy, a person with a preference for red is considered someone who knows how to live well and enjoys good food and drink. This type of person is optimistic, vital, and likes to impress others.

The therapeutic effect of red is stimulating. It is an enhancement to circulation and soothing to sore muscles (the red lamp, for example). Orange-red light on plants stimulates their growth.

79

THE RED GARDEN

Since it is the warmest color, the exuberant color red is enormously conspicuous. In the garden, this effect is further reinforced by the cool, complementary green that is present everywhere. In the garden of the English Hidcote Manor, a double red border has been planted where the red is tempered by many dark red and purplish leaves (see page 78). The conspicuous pure red acquires something mysterious amidst the dark leaves and it balances them out beautifully. The colors are a continuation of each other, so to speak, because they both contain red pigment. This weakens the complementary contrast and, hence, keeps the total picture from being too exciting. A border like this has a totally different character from the blazing yellow-orange-red border of the previous chapter.

Since the warm red colors tend to move into the foreground, a garden with lots of red will seem smaller. Too much red is not very successful in a small garden. In addition, red in the garden has a very stimulating effect on mood. It creates excitement, and we generally go into gardens for peace and quiet! It is therefore best to place a red border in a closed-off area of the garden. If a considerable amount of restful, complementary green is in front of the entrance to this area, the red will be even more of a blaze. Red can also be particularly conspicuous with quantity contrast; when a few red flowers are placed among a profusion of green, they stand out at once.

To avoid the wrong combinations, the color circle divides the group red into "red" and "pure red." "Pure red" is characteristically a warm color and can be combined well with the other sunny colors, yellow and orange. It is sometimes called vermillion red. Pure red can clash badly with red that tends towards red-purple; this will be clear when you think of orange-red combined with pink! "Red" is a somewhat cooler color that contains some blue and borders on red-purple. Light red is red that contains a large amount of white; it is generally called pink. But the makeup of light red is different from that of light red-purple, which is also called pink; look at the color circle to see the difference. This is the reason part of the "pink group" is classified with the color red.

So-called burgundy-red, like that of the *Knautia macedonica*, is not really red but is classified as red-purple.

Right
Border in the Model Gardens with red and white roses, grey-leaved lamb's ears (*Stachys*), and, behind the plants, a screen of lime trees growing as a trellis.

Red is the color of warm blood

Red is the sun in the morning sky

Red is the will that makes us live

Red is everything that must die.

Herko Groot

Left
A combination of pure red, violet, and white produced by Oriental poppies and various irises, in the garden of the painter Claude Monet.

Right [2]
An unusual color combination from the border design used in this chapter is created by the pure red of the annual *Alonsoa,* grey-green of *Artemisia,* and violet of blue vervain *Verbena hastata.*

Top left
The red flowers of the nasturtium *Tropaeolum* "Hermine Grashoff" combine well with the grey of the lead container. A little something extra for the red garden.

Bottom left
White royal lilies among red roses. The red of the roses recurs in the light red stripes on the outside of the royal lily petals.

Right
A white-flowering mullein (*Verbascum*) together with the orange-red columbine *Aquilegia formosa*.

Red in Plant Names

astrosanguineus—dark blood-red
cardinalis—scarlet red
carnea—flesh-colored
coccinea—carmine red
erubescens—light red
ignea—crimson
rosea—rose-red
rubellum—reddish
rubra/ruber—red
sanguineus—blood-red

COMBINATIONS WITH RED

The color red is greatly influenced by other colors in its surroundings. Pure red becomes a blazing color near blue-green leaves but it becomes somewhat dull next to orange. Red is at its most passionate when combined with black. A different aspect of the nature of red shows up with each different color red is placed next to. When combining other colors with red, it is important to determine carefully which kind of red is involved. Red, pure red, and light red all combine perfectly well with white. In the Model Gardens at Lunteren, a wide border has been planted in pure red, white, and many grey-leaved plants. It is a very refreshing combination that includes many red and white roses, as well as red geum (*Geum*), red Texas sage (*Salvia coccinea*), white larkspurs, and the grey of *Artemisia* and *Stachys*. Many (complementary) green leaves make pure red seem particularly intense, and that is why grey leaves are very important here. Woven through the white and intense red of the flowers, they soften the overall effect somewhat. In addition, red shows up beautifully next to grey leaves. The leaves do seem greener because red forces grey towards green, which is its complementary partner. Orange-red becomes a blazing color next to complementary blue-green leaves, for example those of the *Hosta sieboldiana* "Elegans." A somewhat cooler red also matches this color well.

Together with yellow, pure red seems darker and is less exuberant. In the fall, beautiful combinations may be made of late-blooming red flowers or berries together with yellow or orange-brown leaves. The combination with yellow and orange can be seen in the previous chapter. Both red and pure red combine very well with yellow-green, for example red roses with the yellow-green of the annual ornamental tobacco *Nicotiana sanderae* "Limegreen" or a variety of spurge. If a red that tends towards orange is used, the combination with yellow-green becomes somewhat vulgar.

Red with purple and violet is a very rich and daring color combination. Purple especially comes alive next to red and its color shows up beautifully. Or, as Johannes Itten put it, red retreats to become a restrained glow while forcing purple to resist strongly and forcefully. Dark purplish leaves link the colors with each other. The border design in this chapter is based on these colors.

The combination red and blue can be found in the chapter "Color Contrasts."

RED IN LEAVES, BERRIES, AND BARK

A number of plants have red in their leaves, but nowhere is it as intense as in the beet *Beta vulgaris* var. *vulgaris* "Rhubarb Chard," whose color looks beautiful in the red garden. The pure red stalks stand out with great intensity against the complementary, fresh green color of the leaves. Beets are an old-fashioned vegetable whose leaves and stalks can both be eaten. *Houttuynia cordata* "Chameleon" has green leaves with yellow-green and red specks, almost too variegated to be pleasing. Several varieties of Japanese maple, *Acer palmatum*, have dark red leaves and some also have dark purple leaves throughout the summer. These make a beautiful color combination with red flowers. In the fall, more intense colors may be seen. In addition, the variety "Senkaki" has beautiful bright red twigs in winter. The crimson glory vine *Vitis coignetiae* has dark-red-to-almost-black leaves in the fall. Many other plants with dark leaves are discussed in the chapters "Orange" and "Purple."

Before leaves are shed in the fall, they often take on red shades. The smoke tree (*Cotinus*), for example, really stands out then. Red leaves can also be seen in the maple *Acer ginnala*, which is rather small; in the *Acer japonicum* "Aconitifolium," which also has red flowers; in several dogwoods (*Cornus*); in the European spindle tree (*Euonymus*); in the beautiful sweet gum (*Liquidambar*); in Boston ivy (*Parthenocissus*); in the oak *Quercus coccinea* "Splendens"; in the rowanberry *Sorbus hupehensis*; and in various ornamental cherries and apples, which are also decked out with colorful little apples in the fall. The ornamental apple "Gorgeous" is a good variety for the garden since it has lots of shiny little red apples. Edible red berries are produced by the cowberry *Vaccinium vitisidaea*, an excellent ground cover with a beautiful fall color, and of course by the currant (*Ribes rubrum*), which we know from the vegetable garden. The cranberry bush (*Viburnum opulus*) has lots of red berries that make a beautiful color combination with the leaves, whose discoloration tends towards red. The English holly *Ilex aquifolium* "Siberia" is a beautiful variety with lots of bright red berries. Another small plant with red berries is the wintergreen *Gaultheria procumbens*, which is a fragrant ground cover that remains green. The leaves of this little plant take on beautiful shades of orange, red, and purple. Some perennials also take on the red shades of fall, for example the crane's bill *Geranium hhimalayense*.

When, in the winter, all the leaves and fruits have disappeared from the trees and bushes, there still is

Left
In the fall there is a nice combination here of the red-colored leaves of the *Prunus sargentii* that fall to the ground among the intensely red flowers of *Schizostylis coccinea.* The small violet flowers are those of a crocus that blooms in the fall.

Top right
In the fall, the leaves of the grapevine take on the most beautiful red colors and turn the house into something special.

Bottom right
In the fall, the little orange-red apples of the crabapple *Malus* "John Downie" generate lots of color in the garden.

some red to be seen in the garden. The Tartarian dogwood *Cornus alba* "Sibirica," which has intense red twigs, is very conspicuous then. In order for it to continue to produce new, intensely colored branches, this shrub must be pruned every year. Together with *Cornus stolonifera* "Flaviramea,' which has yellow twigs, ornamental grasses and a few remaining perennials, such as the late-flowering *Sedum telephium*, it can be used to create a beautiful winter garden. Somewhat less intense but beautifully brown-red is the shiny trunk of the *Prunus serrula*, a tree that does need a protected spot.

DOUBLE BORDER IN PURE RED, PURPLE, AND VIOLET

This double border with a classical layout has been designed in a color scheme that is not seen very often. It consists of pure red, deep purple, violet, dark leaves, and also some grey-green leaves. It seems mysterious because of the purple and, at the same time, exciting because of the flaming red! If there is enough room, place this color combination in a separate part of the garden. Close off the borders in the back with a tall hedge or isolated shrubs. There is an entrance in the front and two passages through to the left and the right of the pond. If there is less space available, plant one border only. Or use this layout for a different color combination altogether. The two borders have not been planted to be symmetrical, only the lady's-eardrops and the summer lilac have been placed in the same spot on the two sides of the circular pond. Cover the lady's-eardrops with fir branches during winter because this plant is somewhat sensitive to frost.

A walk down the grassy path between the two borders leads to the pond. A red water lily grows in the water. Place an attractive bench near the pond to enjoy the entire garden from that spot. It is easiest to make the pond by placing a preshaped polyester basin in a hollowed-out depression. For water lilies, the depth must be 24–32 in. (60–80 cm.).

Annuals have not been indicated on the layout of plants. Distribute them throughout the border as desired. Excellent choices are the red *Alonsoa meriodionalis*, *Salvia coccinea*, and *Verbena* "Blaze." Additional dark leaves are provided by the orach *Atriplex hortensis* "Red Plume," which can be placed everywhere throughout the border. The perennial *Lobelia fulgens* "Queen Victoria" is very appropriate because of its intensely red flowers and dark leaves. This plant is not winter-hardy and must winter in a frost-free location. Red tulips will produce lots of red in the spring. The red lily *Lilium pumilum* can also be distributed among the perennials. If you have a wall or pergola, a purple *Clematis* would be perfect. Good choices include "Dr. Ruppel," "Gypsy Queen," or "Star of India."

1 Smokebush, *Cotinus coggygria* "Red Beauty"

2 Tartarian dogwood, *Cornus alba* "Sibirica"

3 Rhododendron, *Rhododendron* repens. "Baden-Baden"

4 Summer lilac, *Buddleia davidii* "Border Beauty"

5 Lady's-Eardrops, *Fuchsia* "Riccartonii"

6 Violet x sage, *Salvia superba* "Mainacht"

7 Blue vervain, *Verbena hastata*

8 Sage, *Salvia officinalis* "Berggarten"

9 Montebretia, *Crocosmia* "Lucifer"

10 Anise hyssop, *Agastache foeniculum*

11 Wallflower, *Erysimum* "Bowles Mauve"

12 Bergamot, *Monarda* "Cambridge Scarlet"

13 Red switch grass, *Panicum virgatum* "Rotstrahlbusch"

14 Cinquefoil, *Potentilla* "Gibson's Scarlet"

15 Artemisia, *Artemisia pontica*

16 Weeping willow-leaved pear, *Pyrus salicifolia* "Pendula"

17 Oriental poppy, *Papaver orientale*

18 Rose with large flowers, *Rosa* "Eroica"

19 Summer phlox, *Phlox decussata* "The King"

20 Bellflower, *Campanula lactiflora* "Pouffe"

21 Cotton thistle, *Onopordum bracteatum*

22 Rose with large flowers, *Rosa* "Gisselfeldt"

23 Alumroot, *Heuchera micrantha* "Palace Purple"

24 *Lobelia x gerardii*, "Vedrariensis"

25 Larkspur, *Delphinium* "Elmfreude"

26 Summer phlox, *Phlox decussata* "Blue Evening"

27 Water lily, *Nymphaea* "Escarboucle"

28 Yew, *Taxus baccata*

Design: Modeste Herwig. Measurements: 26 × 33 ft. (8 × 10 m.)

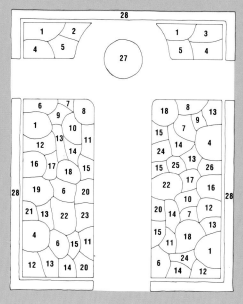

RED TABLE

NAME	COMMON NAME	BLOOM/ MONTHS	LIGHT	HEIGHT IN INCHES	TYPE	PLANTS PER YD²	NOTES
Acer japonicum "Aconitifolium"	Japanese maple	4–5	○ ◐	20–30 ft			red autumn color
Achillea millefolium "Fanal"	Common yarrow	6–8	○ ◐	20–30	○	7	red
Adonis aestivalis	Pheasant's eye	5–8	○	10–20	⊙	9	pure red
Alonsoa meridionalis		7–9	○	10–20	⊙	9–11	pure red
Aquilegia formosa	Columbine	5–6	○ ◐	30–40	○	9	red-orange and yellow
Astilbe arendsii "Glow"	Spiraea	7–8	○ ◐	20–30	○	5–7	red
Astilbe japonica "Red Sentinel"	Spiraea	7–8	○ ◐	20–30	○	7	red
Astilbe simplicifolia "Inshriach Pink"	Spiraea	7–8	○ ◐	8–16	○	7	light red
Beta vulgaris "Rhubarb Chard"			○ ◐	8–16	○	5–7	pure-red leaf stalks
Canna indica "President"	Indian-shot	7–10	○	30–40	⊛	5	pure red; not winter hardy
Centranthus ruber	Red valerian	5–7	○	20–30	○	5	red
Cornus alba "Sibirica"	Tartarian dogwood	5–6	○ ◐	to 10 ft	⊛	1	pure red branches
Crocosmia "Lucifer"	Montbretia	7–9	○	20–40	⊛	5–7	pure red; sensitive to frost
Dahlia "Chat Noir"		7–10	○	30–40	⊛	5–7	red
Delphinium ruysii "Pink Sensation"		6–7	○	40–50	○	5–7	light red
Filipendula rubra "Venusta Magnifica"	Queen-of-the-prairie	7–8	○ ◐	to 8 ft	○	5–7	light red
Fuchsia "Riccartonii"	Lady's-eardrops	6–9	○	30–50	⊛	1–2	red; purple calyx
Gaultheria procumbens	Wintergreen	7–8	◐ ◑	6–8	⊛	9–11	red berries; ground cover
Geum "Red Wings"	Avens	5–7	○ ◐	12–24	○	7	pure red
Geum chiloense "Mrs. Bradshaw"	Avens	5–7	○ ◐	10–20	○	7	pure red
Geum coccineum "Feuermeer"	Avens	5–7	○ ◐	10–20	○	7	red-orange
Hamamelis intermedia "Diane"	Witch hazel	1–2	○ ◐	to 13 ft	⊛		red
Hemerocallis "Stafford"	Day lily	6–8	○ ◐	20–30	○	3–5	red
Heuchera brizoides "Pluie de Feu"	Alum root	7–8	○ ◐	10–20	○	7	red
Ilex aquifolium "Siberia"	English holly	5–6	○ ◐ ◑	to 50 ft	⊛	1	pure red berries
Imperata cylindrica "Red Baron"			○ ◐	25–50	○	9	red-grey ornamental grass
Lilium "Red Carpet"	Lily	7–8	○ ◐	35–40	⊚	9–11	pure red
Lilium pumilum	Coral lily	7–8	○ ◐	20–30	⊚	9–11	pure red
Liquidambar styraciflua	Sweet gum	5	○	to 33 ft	⊛		red-orange autumn color
Lobelia cardinalis	Cardinal flower	7–9	○	40–60	○	7	pure red; not winter hardy
Lobelia fulgens "Queen Victoria"		8–10	○	40–60	○	7	pure red; dark leaves
Lupinus "My Castle"	Lupine	6–7	○ ◐	30–40	○	3	red
Lychnis chalcedonica	Maltese cross	6–7	○ ◐	40–50	○	5–7	pure red
Mimulus "Scarlet Bees"		6–8	○ ◐	25–50	○	7	red; cultivated as an annual
Monarda "Cambridge Scarlet"		7–9	○ ◐	30–50	○	7	pure red
Nymphaea "Escarboucle"		6–9	○		○	1	plant at a depth of 16–32 inches
Papaver glaucum	Tulip poppy	6–7	○	20–30	⊙	9	pure red
Papaver orientale	Oriental poppy	5–6	○ ◐	20–40	○	5	pure red
Papaver rhoeas	Corn poppy	5–7	○ ◐	16–24	⊙	9–11	pure red
Parthenocissus tricuspidata	Boston ivy		○ ◐	to 50 ft	⊛	1	climber; red autumn color
Phlox drummondii	Star phlox	7–9	○	10–20	⊙	9–11	red; butterfly plant
Phlox paniculata "Rosa Pastell"	Summer phlox	7–9	○ ◐	50–60	○	5–7	light red
Phygelius capensis "Coccineus"	Cape fuchsia	7–10	○	30–40	⊛	9	pure red; not winter hardy
Polygonum affine "Darjeeling Red"	Knotweed	7–9	○ ◐	4–10	○	7	light red; ground cover
Polygonum amplexicaule "Roseum"	Mountain fleece	7–11	○ ◐	40–60	○	3	light red
Polygonum bistorta	Snakeweed	5–8	○ ◐	30–40	○	3	light red
Potentilla "Flamenco"	Cinquefoil	6–8	○	10–20	○	7	pure red
Potentilla "Gibson's Scarlet"	Cinquefoil	6–8	○	10–20	○	7	pure red
Prunus serrula		4–5	○	to 25 ft	⊛		red-grey outer bark
Pulmonaria rubra	Lungwort	4–5	◐ ◑	10	⊛	7–9	light red
Quercus coccinea "Splendens"	Scarlet oak		○	to 80 ft	⊛		red autumn color
Rhododendron knaphill-exbury "Cecile"	Azalea	5–6	○ ◐	50–70	⊛	1	light red
Rhododendron knaphill-exbury "Satan"	Azalea	5–6	○ ◐	50–70	⊛	1	pure red
Rhododendron repens "Baden-Baden"	Rhododendron	5	◐	to 5 ft	⊛	2–3	pure red
Ricinus communis "Impala"	Castor bean	8–9	○	to 15 ft	⊙	1–2	dark leaves with red veins
Rosa "Blessings"	Rose	6–10	○	30–50	⊛	3	light red
Rosa "Chimo"	Rose bush	6–9	○	to 8 ft	⊛	1	pure red
Rosa "Eroica (Erotika)"	Rose	6–10	○	30–50	⊛	3	pure red

NAME	COMMON NAME	BLOOM/ MONTHS	LIGHT	HEIGHT IN INCHES	TYPE	PLANTS PER YD²	NOTES
Rosa "Gisselfeldt"	Rose	6–10	○	30–50	⬤	3	pure red
Rosa "Havam (Amsterdam)"	Polyanthus rose	6–10	○	30–50	⬤	3	pure red
Rosa "John Waterer"	Rose	6–10	○	30–50	⬤	3	pure red
Rosa "Kolima (Lilli Marlene)"	Polyanthus rose	6–10	○	30–50	⬤	3	pure red
Rosa "Macci (City of Belfast)"	Polyanthus rose	6–10	○	30–50	⬤	3	pure red
Rosa "New Daily Mail (Pussta)"	Polyanthus rose	6–10	○	30–50	⬤	3	pure red
Rosa "New Dawn"	Climbing rose	6–9	○	to 10 ft	⬤	1	light red
Rosa "Parkdirektor Riggers"	Climbing rose	6–10	○	to 10 ft	⬤	1	pure red
Rosa "Pernille Poulsen"	Climbing rose	6–10	○	30–50	⬤	3	light red
Rosa "Tojo"	Climbing rose	6–10	○	30–50	⬤	3	pure red
Rosa "Zwergkönigin"	Miniature rose	6–10	○	16–24	⬤	3–5	pure red
Salvia coccinea	Texas sage	6–10	○	20–30	○	7	pure red
Skimmia japonica "Rubella"		4–5	◑	to 5 ft	⬤	3	red flower buds in winter
Tropaeolum "Hermine Grashoff"		7–10	○ ◑	8–12	☉	5–7	pure red
Tulipa "Carlton"	Tulip	4–5	○	8–12	◉	15–20	pure red
Tulipa "Couleur Cardinal"	Tulip	4–5	○	8–12	◉	15–20	red
Tulipa greigii "Roodkapje"	Tulip	4–5	○	8–12	◉	15–20	pure red
Tulipa praestans "Fusilier"	Tulip	4	○	8–12	◉	15–20	orange-red
Verbena "Blaze"		6–10	○	8–12	☉	9–11	pure red
Vitis coignetiae	Crimson glory vine	6–7	○	to 40 ft	⬤	1	red-grey autumn color

○ full sun; ◑ partial shade; ● shade
◉ perennial plant; ☉ biennial; ☉ annual; ◉ bulb; ⓣ tuber; ⬤ shrub; ● tree

Red roses combined with yellow and dark leaves in the garden of Penelope Hobhouse. Next to the dark color of the leaves the red stands out less.

89

RED-PURPLE

Left
A cozy corner on the terrace with red-purple *Pelargonium* in front of the window and with *Buxus,* heather, and an ornamental cabbage planted in pots.

The rich red-purple of the Chinese peony, *Paeonia officinales* "China Rose."

Red-purple is not a spectral color, and most books about color theories do not discuss this color. It is situated in between red and purple, as the name indicates. But it is a common color in flowers and in this book I intentionally devote considerable attention to this marvelous color.

Light red-purple, i.e., pink, is considered a feminine color. According to a well-known color psychologist, two out of three women like red-purple. And I think that there must be some truth in this. In the Model Gardens at Lunteren, female visitors are very enthusiastic about the red-purple area around the big pond.

Intense, saturated red-purple is a very conspicuous color. In the 1930s this color even had a provocative effect when it began to be used in clothing after white had been the predominantly used color. The fashion designer Schiaparelli introduced intense pink as "shocking pink." During the 1950s "hot pink" was the preferred color in fashion. It was the latest craze and was encouraged by fashion magazines and also by the musical *Funny Face* with Audrey Hepburn. "Think Pink," one of the songs in this movie, is entirely about pink. In the 1960s red-purple was fashionable, but as a "crazy color."

A pronounced shade of red-purple is very luxurious, happy, and exciting. It is a color that is attractive to children. This is the reason many candies are pink. Light shades of this color are lovely and soft, for example the pink blossoms that can be seen in the spring when orchards are blooming exuberantly. But even this color has negative meanings; it may mean cloying and meaninglessness; it may suggest a goody-goody and, sometimes also, a loud color.

THE RED-PURPLE GARDEN

Red-purple is an excellent color for making a monochromatic (one-color) border. Many flowers have this attractive, happy color and so there is a wide selection. The more intense shades of this color are often called "cyclamen-colored" and "fuchsia." I once designed a garden with bright red-purple flowers, such as purple loosestrife (*Lythrum*) and purple coneflower (*Echinacea*), together with grey-leaved plants and many ornamental grasses. It is often very beautiful, especially in a small garden, to have one color only. Different degrees of saturation of the red-purple (quality contrast) provide variation.

A garden in light red-purple has a totally different mood. Its effect is peaceful and quiet, but it may also become expressionless. In order to bring out the beauty of the soft pastel color, it is important to have dark shades of other colors in the surroundings, for example dark green leaves. In front of his light red-purple house with blue-green shutters, the painter Monet had planted light red-purple Chinese peonies and also dark red-purple flowers. The dark green leaves surrounding the flowers and the bright blue-green of the house produced a beautiful combination with the red-purple (see the top photo on page 97).

Grey-leaved plants are also indispensable in the red-purple garden because they contribute greatly to making the flowers stand out. When using light colors, it is important to place the plants in distinctive groups for structure in the overall image. Contrasts of shape may be helpful in producing structure and also straight lines in the layout of the garden. Before planting a light red-purple border that will be fully exposed to the sun, keep in mind that this light color may become very dull in the intense light. Light red-purple looks better in half-shade.

You can create a light-dark contrast by combining red-purple with a lighter variation of the same color. An example can be seen in the photo of the rose "Fantin Latour" together with the *Clematis* "Julia Correvon," very romantic indeed!

Left
A romantic combination in one color consisting of dark red-purple *Clematis* "Madame Jules Correvon" and, in a lighter side of the same color, the rose "Fantin Latour."

Top right
A red-purple corner in the herb garden at Sissinghurst with foxglove and honeysuckle.

Bottom right
This combination is at its most beautiful in the late summer. The intense red-purple flowers of the mountain-fleece *Polygonum amplexicaule* stand out beautifully next to the black of the pergola. A subdued shade of the red-purple recurs in the panicles of the eulalia *Miscanthus sinensis* "Malepartus."

Top left
A spring combination in white and red-purple of late-flowering tulips and the *Triandus narcissus* "Thalia."

Left (second from top)
A combination of soft pastels of light red-purple flowers of the *Rosa* "Perle d'Or" and, below these, the fleabane *Erigeron karvinskianus*

Left (second from bottom)
The primrose *Primula x bullesiana* displays a subtle combination of yellow and red-purple.

Bottom left
Endless combinations can be made with red-purple, purple, and violet. Here the light red-purple rose "Pink Parfait" is combined with violets in various shades of violet.

Right
No intense colors have been used in this border at Piet Oudolf's nursery. A natural impression is conveyed by red-purple, violet, and white.

COMBINATIONS WITH RED-PURPLE

Red-purple is an easy color to make combinations with. All the colors between red-purple and yellow as well as certain shades of red can be used. Only orange and pure red do not go well with this color. The combination of red-purple and yellow is possible, but it depends on the specific shades used whether or not it will be really successful. For more about this see the chapter "Combinations with Contrasting Colors."

Due to the simultaneous contrast, red-purple seems redder next to green, and this makes it more expressive. Light red-purple especially should be helped by a large amount of dark green and other sturdy colors to keep it from becoming too sweet. Next to grey-green and blue-green leaves, red-purple flowers look very sophisticated. For example, a very pleasing effect is obtained by planting the non-winter-hardy *Helichrysum petiolare* in a pot together with the soft red-purple bindweed *Convolvulus cantibrica*. Grey-colored tiles or other hard materials also go well with red-purple flowers. In Monet's garden in Giverny, the espaliers have been painted blue-green and make a beautiful color combination with the red-purple roses that grow in abundance (see page 37). The dark color of grey-purple leaves also goes well with red-purple flowers. The rose *Rosa glauca* is a beautiful example of the presence of this color combination in one and the same plant. In late summer, however, this rose produces small red hips that may clash with the red-purple color scheme.

White is very refreshing next to red-purple. The lighter shades of red-purple seem darker next to bright white and are therefore more conspicuous. Some flowers make color combinations with these colors on their own; an example is the *Phlox* (Maculata-hybr.) "Omega," which has white flowers with a red-purple disk.

In her grey garden, Gertrude Jekyll used much light red-purple, white, and purple-violet, in addition to the grey-leaved plants. This is a beautiful, soft combination of colors that stimulate each other.

Endless combinations can be made with red-purple, purple, violet, and all the colors in between. These colors are located in the same area of the color circle and do not easily clash with each other. Very romantic plant designs can be made with these colors, or use intense colors to make very exciting combinations.

The combination red-purple with blue is discussed in the chapter "Blue" because red-purple is indispensable in a blue garden.

RED-PURPLE IN LEAVES AND BERRIES

Plants with some red-purple in their leaves fit beautifully in a red-purple garden. There are red-purple specks in the leaves of the carpet bugleweed *Ajuga reptans* "Burgundy Glow." In colorful surroundings, these extremely variegated leaves easily become flashy, but in a quiet setting they may create nice accents. The climbing kiwi *Actinidia kolomikta* has very unusual leaves: the bottom half is green and the other half is creamy white and red-purple. But in a cool summer, the discoloration may be disappointing. In a red-purple garden, this plant looks beautiful against a fence or wall facing south.

In the fall, the leaves of the winged spindle tree *Euonymus alatus* turn a beautiful red-purple. The fruits of several varieties of the spindle tree are also red-purple. The large berries of the *Pernettya mucronata*, a small evergreen shrub that is not very winter-hardy, are a really intense red-purple. The female plants produce berries only if there is a male plant nearby. The pokeweed (*Phytolacca*), which grows in a rather uncontrolled manner, produces dark red-purple berries that are sometimes almost black; they grow on stems that have an intense red-purple color. The juice of its poisonous berries is of the same color and is strong enough to be used as a dye but, unfortunately, not easy to fix. Until late in the fall, the variety of rowanberry called *Sorbus hupehensis* "November Pink" continues to produce light red-purple berries while also showing beautiful fall foliage.

Top left
In the fall, winged spindle tree *Euonymus alatus* leaves turn an incredibly intense red-purple.

Center left
In warm summers, the top half of the *Actinidia kolomikta* leaves are red-purple. Here, it grows against a wall with a *Clematis* with large flowers.

Bottom left
The bright red-purple of the rose "Baron Girod de l'Ain" with the violet-blue of the *Geranium pratense* "Mrs. Kendall Clark."

Top right
In Monet's garden at Giverny, the red-purple of the Chinese peonies recurs in the color of the house, just barely seen through the trees.

Bottom right
Light shades of red-purple stand out next to grey-green leaves, seen here in the combination of the *Lavandula angustifolia* "Rosea" and the grey-leaved *Santolina chamaecyparissus*.

A BORDER IN RED-PURPLE

The border design in this chapter is by Ton ter Linden, who has planted marvelous gardens in the town of Ruinen, in the province of Drenthe, in the Netherlands. Among these are several beautiful gardens based on color and many wide, colorful borders.

The splendid, sophisticated combinations in this border are the result of Ton ter Linden's excellent feel for colors. The main color, red-purple, is supported in various places by shades of violet and the grey-purple leaves of the orach *Atriplex hortensis* "Red Plume." Insert this annual in the overall design following your own ideas. Once the orach has been planted, do not worry about losing this plant, since it spreads its seeds in abundance. The delicate grey-green of artemisias gives a finishing touch to the border. Light and dark shades of red-purple alternate. This can be seen, for example, where the beautiful rose "Dainty Bess," which has single light red-purple flowers, stands above the *Teucrium marum* with its more intense color. In the back of the rather narrow border are large groups of tall plants, while smaller groups of lower plants with a more delicate texture are placed more towards the front. This gives a clear structure to this border with its tender colors.

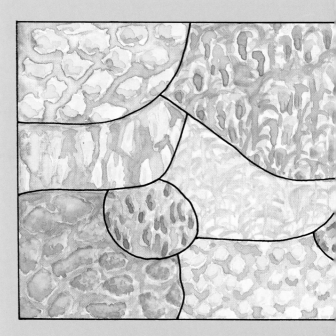

The beautiful rose "Dainty Bess" (shown here together with love-in-a-mist) was chosen by Ton ter Linden for the border design used in this chapter.

Pink and Fragrant

The romantic rose is not only pleasing to the eye but also very fragrant. One of the most fragrant roses is the damask rose *Rosa damascena* "Trigintipetala," which has been cultivated for hundreds of years for the production of the precious attar of roses. The attar is extremely expensive because over 1500 lb (700 kilo) of rose petals only produce slightly over two lb. (one kilo) of attar of roses.

DESIGN AND LIST OF PLANTS

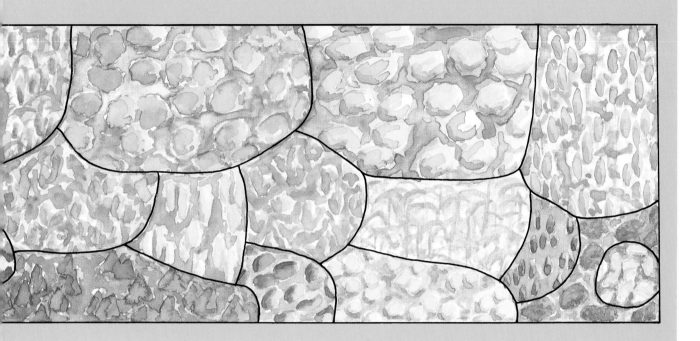

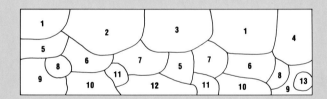

1 Bergamot, *Monarda* "Beauty of Cobham"

2 Speedwell, *Veronica virginica* "Fascination"

3 Summer phlox, *Phlox decussata* "Rosa Spier"

4 Horsemint, *Mentha longifolia* "Buddleia"

5 Mallow, *Sidalcea* "Elsie Heugh"

6 Artemisia, *Artemisia ludoviciana* "Silver Queen"

7 Obedience, *Physostegia virginiana* "Bouquet Rose"

8 Blue vervain, *Verbena hastata*

9 Germander, *Teucrium marum*

10 Crane's bill, *Geranium oxonianum* "Rose Clair"

11 Meadow rue, *Thalictrum rochebrunianum*

12 Spirea, *Astilbe* arendsii "Glow"

13 Rose with large flowers, *Rosa* "Dainty Bess"

Design: Ton ter Linden. Measurements: 23 × 6½ ft. (7 × 2 m.)

RED-PURPLE TABLE

NAME	COMMON NAME	BLOOM/ MONTHS	LIGHT	HEIGHT IN INCHES	TYPE	PLANTS PER YD²	NOTES
Achillea "Heidi"	Common yarrow	6–8	○◐	20–30	○	7	
Achillea millefolium "Summer Wine"	Common yarrow	6–8	○◐	20–30	○	7	dark red-purple
Achillea "Weser River Sandstone"	Common yarrow	6–8	○◐	20–30	○	7	dark red-purple
Actinidia kolomikta		6	○	to 7 ft	⊛	1	green/red-purple leaves
Ajuga reptans "Burgundy Glow"	Carpet bugleweed	5–6	◐	6–8	○	9–11	leaves with red-purple spots
Allium cernuum	Wild onion	6–7	○	20–30	⊚	12–16	
Allium christophii	Stars-of-Persia	5–6	○	10–20	⊚	9–11	
Anemone lesseri	Anemone	5–6	○◐	10–20	○	9	
Aquilegia vulgaris "Nora Barlow"		5–6	○◐	20–30	○	9	red-purple with green
Armeria maritima	Thrift	5–6	○	4–8	○	9–11	dry soil
Aster ericoides "Esther"	Heath aster	9–10	○	20–30	○	7	light red-purple
Aster novi-belgii "Crimson Brocade"	Michaelmas daisy	9–10	○	50–60	○	5	butterfly plant
Astilbe arendsii "Spinell"	Spiraea	7–8	○◐	20–30	○	5–7	
Astilbe japonica "Düsseldorf"	Spiraea	7–8	○◐	20–30	○	5–7	
Astilbe simplicifolia "Aphrodite"	Spiraea	7–8	○◐	10–20	○	7	light red-purple
Astrantia major "Rubra"	Masterwort	6–8	○◐	20–30	○	7	
Astrantia major involucrata "Canneman"	Masterwort	6–8	○◐	20–30	○	7	turns green as it wilts
Astrantia maxima	Masterwort	6–8	○◐	20–30	○	7	light red-purple
Berberis thunbergii "Rose Glow"	Japanese barberry	5–6	○	to 7 ft	⊛	1	red-purple leaves
Bergenia "Morgenröte"		4–5	◐	20–30	○	5	foliage plant
Buddleia davidii "Pink Delight"	Summer lilac	7–9	○	to 15 ft	⊛		prune back in spring
Campanula lactiflora "Loddon Anna"	Bellflower	6–8	○◐	30–40	○	7	light red-purple
Centaurea montana "Carnea"	Mountain bluet	5–8	○◐	10–20	○	5–7	light red-purple
Cirsium rivulare "Atropurpureum"		6–7	○	30–40	○	5	dark red-purple
Clematis "Comtesse de Bouchaud"	Virgin's bower	7–8	○◐	to 10 ft	⊛	1	climber
Clematis "Madame Jules Correvon"		7–9	○◐	to 10 ft	⊛	1	climber
Clematis montana "Elizabeth"	Virgin's bower	5–6	○◐	to 27 ft	⊛	1	climber
Cleome spinosa "Rose Queen"	Spider plant	7–10	○	40–50	⊙	5	
Convolvulus cantabrica	Bindweed	6–8	○	10–20	○	3–5	not winter hardy
Crinum powellii	Crinum lily	7–9	○	20–30	⊚	5	not winter hardy
Deutzia hybrida "Contraste"		6	○◐	40–60	⊛	1	light red-purple
Dianthus gratianopolitanus "Pink Jewel"	Cheddar pink	4–5	○	4–6	○	9–11	grey-green leaves
Dianthus plumarius "Maggie"	Cottage pink	5–6	○	4–6	○	9–11	
Diascia barberae	Twinspur	7–9	○	8–12	○	9–11	not winter hardy; light red-purple
Diascia "Ruby Fields"	Twinspur	7–9	○	8–12	○	9–11	not winter hardy
Dicentra formosa	Western bleeding-heart	5–8	◐	8–12	○	7–9	grey-green leaves
Dictamnus albus	Dittany	6–7	○	30–40	○	5	
Echinacea purpurea	Purple coneflower	7–9	○	20–30	○	7	butterfly plant
Euonymus alata	Winged spindle tree	5–6	○◐	to 7 ft	⊛	1	red-purple autumn colors
Filipendula purpurea	Meadowsweet	7–8	○◐	20–30	○	5–7	intense red-purple
Geranium endressii "Wargrave Pink"	Cranesbill	5–8	○◐	8–16	○	7	light red-purple
Geranium oxonianum "Rose Clair"		6–8	○◐	10–20	○	5–7	light red-purple
Geranium phaeum	Cranesbill	6–7	○◐	20	○	5	dark red-purple
Geranium psilostemon	Cranesbill	6–7	○◐	20–30	○	3–5	intense red-purple
Geranium sanguineum "Jubilee Pink"	Cranesbill	5–8	○◐	10	○	5–7	light red-purple
Gypsophila repens "Pink Star"		5–7	○	4	○	5–7	
Helleborus orientalis	Lenten rose	3–4	○◐	10–20	○	7	
Hydrangea macrophylla "Bouquet Rose"	French hydrangea	7	○◐	to 7 ft	⊛	1	
Indigofera amblyantha	Indigo	7–10	○	to 6 ft	⊛	1	needs a protected location
Knautia macedonica		7–9	○	20–30	○	5	dark red-purple
Kolkwitzia amabilis		5–6	○	to 15 ft	⊛	1	
Lamium maculatum "Shell Pink"	Spotted beauty bush	6–8	◐●	6–10	○	7–9	light red-purple; ground cover
Lathyrus odoratus "Radar"	Sweet pea	6–10	○	to 6 ft	⊙	3–5	fragrant; climber
Lathyrus vernus	Spring vetchling	4–5	◐	10–20	○	5–7	
Lavatera "Barnsley"	Tree mallow	7–11	○	60–70	○	1–3	sensitive to frost
Lavatera trimestris "Silver Cup"	Tree mallow	6–9	○	30–40	⊙	5–7	
Lilium "Cote d'Azur"	Lily	7–8	○◐	30–40	⊚	9–11	
Linaria purpurea "Canon J. Went"	Spurred snapdragon	5–9	○	30–40	○	7	light red-purple

NAME	COMMON NAME	BLOOM/ MONTHS	LIGHT	HEIGHT IN INCHES	TYPE	PLANTS PER YD²	NOTES
Lonicera periclymenum "Serotina"	Woodbine	6–9	○ ◐	to 13 ft	shrub	1	climber; red berries
Lupinus "Abendglut"	Lupine	6–7	○ ◐	30–40	○	3	
Lythrum salicaria	Purple loosestrife	6–8	○ ◐ ●	30–60	○	5	
Magnolia quinquepeta "Nigra"		5–6	○ ◐ ●	to 10 ft	shrub		dark red-purple
Magnolia soulangiana "Lennei"	Chinese magnolia	4–5	○ ◐ ●	to 23 ft	shrub		
Malope trifida "Rosea"		7–10	○	24–32	⊙	5	
Malus (c) "Liset"	Crab apple	5	○	to 20 ft	tree		grey-purple leaves
Monarda "Beauty of Cobham"	Bergamot	7–9	○ ◐	30–50	○	7	light red-purple
Monarda "Fishes"	Bergamot	7–9	○ ◐	30–50	○	7	light red-purple
Monarda "Kardinal"	Bergamot	7–9	○ ◐	30–50	○	7	
Montia sibirica	Siberian purslane	4–7	◐	4–6	○	7–9	
Nicotiana sanderae "Crimson Bedder"		6–10	○ ◐	20–30	⊙	9–11	
Paeonia lactiflora "Bowl of Beauty"	Chinese peony	6	○	20–30	○	3	light red-purple; single flowers
Paeonia lactiflora "Sarah Bernhardt"	Chinese peony	6	○	20–30	○	3	with many petals
Papaver orientale "Karine"	Oriental poppy	6–7	○ ◐	20–30	○	5	light red-purple
Pernettya mucronata		5–6	◐	20–30	shrub	5	red-purple berries
Phlox paniculata "Rijnstroom"	Summer phlox	7–9	○ ◐	50–60	○	5–7	
Phlox paniculata "Rosa Spier"	Summer phlox	7–9	○ ◐	50–60	○	5–7	light red-purple
Phuopsis stylosa		6–8	○ ◐	6–12	○	9–11	rock garden plant
Platycodon grandiflorus "Perlmutterschale"	Balloon flower	7–8	○ ◐	20–30	○	9	light red-purple
Polygonum affine "Dimity"	Knotweed	7–9	○ ◐	4–10	○	7	ground cover
Polygonum amplexicaule "Speciosum"	Mountain-fleece	7–11	○ ◐	40–60	○	3	
Primula japonica	Japanese primrose	5–6	◐	20–30	○	7–9	
Primula Bullesiana	Primrose	6–7	◐	20–30	○	7–9	red purple with orange-yellow
Rhododendron "Rosalind"	Japanese azalea	5–6	◐	20–30	shrub	2–3	
Rhododendron "Sylphides"	Azalea	5–6	○ ◐	50–70	shrub	1	
Rhododendron praecox	Rhododendron	2–3	○ ◐	to 4 ft	shrub	1–2	
Rosa "Anneke Doorenbos"	Polyanthus rose	6–10	○	30–50	shrub	3	
Rosa "Bantry Bay"	Climbing rose	6–9	○	to 10 ft	shrub	1	
Rosa "Constance Spry"	Climbing rose	6–7	○	to 10 ft	shrub	1	light red-purple; fragrant
Rosa "Dainty Bess"	Rose	6–10	○	30–50	shrub	3	light red purple; single flowers
Rosa "Interlada (Lady of the Dawn)"	Polyanthus rose	6–10	○	30–50	shrub	3	light red-purple to white
Rosa "Pink Fringe"	Polyanthus rose	6–10	○	30–50	shrub	3	ruffled petals
Rosa "Queen Elizabeth"	Rose	6–10	○	30–50	shrub	3	
Rosa "Raubritter"	Rose	6–8	○	30–50	shrub	3	light red-purple
Rosa "The Fairy"	Rose	6–10	○	20–30	shrub	3–5	light red-purple
Rosa "Veilchenblau"	Climbing rose	6–7	○	to 10 ft	shrub	1	almost purple!
Rosa "Zéphirine Drouhin"	Climbing rose	7–9	○	to 10 ft	shrub	1	without thorns
Rosa centifolia "Fantin-Latour"	Cabbage rose	6–8	○	to 7 ft	shrub	1	light red-purple
Rosa damascena	Damask rose	6–7	○	to 7 ft	shrub	1	fragrant
Rosa "Heritage"	Rose	6–9	○	to 7 ft	shrub	1	fragrant
Rosa glauca	Rose	6–7	○	to 10 ft	shrub	1	grey-purple leaves
Salvia nemorosa "Brightness"	Sage	6–8	○ ◐	20–30	○	7	
Salvia x superba "Rose Queen"	Sage	6–8	○ ◐	20–30	○	7	
Salvia viridis "Pink Gem"	Sage	6–9	○ ◐	10–20	⊙	7–9	
Sanguisorba obtusa	Burnet	7–9	○ ◐	30–40	○	3–5	
Saxifraga urbium "Clarence Elliott"	London-pride	6–7	◐ ●	4–10	○	9	
Sedum "Autumn Joy"		8–9	○ ◐	20	○	7	turns brown; butterfly plant
Sedum "Robustum"		7–8	○ ◐	8–16	○	7	grey-purple leaves; butterfly plant
Sedum spectabile "Brillant"	Stonecrop	8–9	○ ◐	10–20	○	7	butterfly plant
Sidalcea "Elsie Heugh"	Mallow	7–9	○	30–40	○	7	light red-purple
Sidalcea "Mr. Lindbergh"	Mallow	7–9	○	30–40	○	7	
Spiraea bumalda "Antony Waterer"	Spirea	7–9	○	20–30	shrub	3	
Syringa vulgaris "Katherine Havemeyer"	Common lilac	5–6	○ ◐	to 13 ft	shrub	1	light red-purple; double flowers
Tulipa aucherana	Tulip	4–5	○	2	bulb	20–25	
Tulipa "Angelique"	Tulip	5–6	○	40	bulb	15–20	light red-purple
Tulipa "Peach Blossom"	Tulip	4–5	○	8–12	bulb	15–20	light red-purple
Veronica spicata "Red Fox"	Speedwell	6–8	○	16–24	○	7	
Veronicastrum virginicum "Roseum"	Speedwell	7–8	○	50–70	○	5	light red-purple
Weigela "Feerei"		5–6	○ ◐	to 10 ft	shrub	1	light red-purple

○ full sun; ◐ partial shade; ● shade
○ perennial plant; ⊙ biennial; ○ annual; bulb; tuber; shrub; tree

PURPLE

Left
The flowers of the nettle *Stachys grandiflora,* with their delicate markings, are set off beautifully here against the background of lavender buds.

The purple knapweed *Centaurea dealbata* combined with the beard-tongue *Penstemon* "Sour Grapes."

Purple is an impressive color. Located between red and blue, it has something of the nature of each of these two colors. Like red, deep purple is exciting and warm but, at the same time, it also has some of the mystery of blue. Since this color is produced by mixing the masculine red and the feminine blue, it is considered the color of love and of the goddess Venus. In Shakespeare's play *Antony and Cleopatra,* the sails of the boat belonging to this sensual and imperious Egyptian queen were purple. In an erotic garden there should be many plants with purple flowers!

Purple is the complementary color to yellow, the color of knowledge and intellect, and is therefore considered the color of the unconscious and the mysterious. Dark purple can even be threatening. A light shade is much gentler.

Since purple dye used to be extremely expensive, only the rich could wear purple clothing. Purple dye, the Tyrrhenian purple, was obtained from the sea slug *Purpurea haemastoma,* from which the word purple is derived. Royal purple, the color of clothing worn by emperors and kings, was a rather reddish purple. In the Catholic Church, it is the color of penance as well as the color of the bishop's clothing. It is the color of the ruler and of all that is sublime, but it is also the color of the despot and of decadence.

In 1865, a much cheaper, synthetic version of purple dye was invented. Ever since, purple, light purple especially, has been an important color in fashion. It was called lilac or mauve, after the French name for the plant *Malva.* During the 1960s, purple was often combined with vivid orange, both in interiors and in clothing, to achieve a psychedelic effect.

In color therapy, people with a preference for purple are considered lighthearted, cheerful, and interested in whatever is unusual.

THE PURPLE GARDEN

A garden with only green leaves and dark purple flowers will convey the impression of darkness and gloom. Purple is the darkest color (see the chart on page 24) and does not stand out much. To make the deep purple of flowers attractive, surround them with light-colored flowers for a light-dark contrast. For example, make a beautiful monochromatic border with various shades of light and dark purple using dark larkspurs and sage together with light purple *Phlox* and clary. Grey-green leaves are attractive in a purple garden. Grey-green, a light, neutral color, makes the purple much livelier.

The nature of purple depends on the proportion of red and blue, the two colors purple is located between.

The greater the proportion of red, the warmer the purple will be and the more it will stand out. When blue is dominant, purple will be a much cooler color. Use different shades of purple intentionally to introduce variety in a purple garden. This was done in the splendid purple border at Sissinghurst, where a little light red-purple was used to make the dark purple more lively. The *Clematis* trailing up along the old wall provides a purple background in summer.

Light purple and grey-green in quantity make a garden seem bigger. The rather cool, soft color of light purple is not obtrusive and conveys a feeling of restfulness to the entire garden. Add to this light color some dark tones to keep the overall picture from becoming too pale. Dark green or dark, purplish leaves provide a beautiful background. In the intense yellow light of the sun, light purple is less appropriate because all the color quickly disappears.

Left
A beautiful container with the annual *Ageratum houstonianum* in the garden of Wakehurst Place in England. The attention is immediately focused on the purple precisely because, proportionately, it only covers a small area (quantity contrast).

Top right
Various varieties of virgin's-bower (*Clematis*) grow against the old wall that stands behind the purple border in Sissinghurst.

Bottom right
Flowers can be very decorative even when they have finished flowering, as in the case of these flowers of an ornamental onion plant that stick out above the beard-tongue, *Penstemon* "Sour Grapes."

Top left
The grey-green leaves of the white *Senecio bicolor* look beautiful next to the light purple virgin's-bower *Clematis* "H.F. Young," which is seen here covering the ground as a creeper.

Center left
The wild pansy (or love-in-idleness) *Viola tricolor,* which has the colors yellow, purple, and violet in its small flowers, looks just beautiful when placed on a table in a basket like this one.

Bottom left
The flowers of the hollyhock (*Alcea rosea nigra*) are grey-purple, which means that the purple contains some black.

Right
The large purple spherical heads of the onion *Allium christophii* show up beautifully next to the delicate flowers of the love-in-a-mist.

COMBINATIONS WITH PURPLE

The blue/red proportions of the purple as well as its brightness must be taken into account also when making combinations. Deep purple seems even darker next to white, and this keeps the color from showing up well. Cream-colored flowers are a much better choice because they have a lower degree of brightness. The beautiful phlox *Phlox decussata* "Wilhelm Kesselring" produces this combination on its own. It has purple petals and a white disk and goes together very beautifully with less conspicuous, sparsely growing plants.

The combination purple with red has been discussed in the chapter "Red." The border design presented in that chapter is done in these colors.

There is no end to the number of combinations with purple and red-purple. Light and dark shades, those approaching violet, and those tending toward red all mix well. There is an enormous selection of plants with flowers in these colors. Beautiful pastel-colored combinations can be made with light purple, light red-purple, and grey-green leaves. You could, for example, combine the light red-purple toadflax *Linaria purpurea* "Canon J. Went" with the light purple *Galega officinalis*. You could also have the light shades recur in flowers with more pronounced colors or create accents with contrasting colors or use the same flowers in several places to create an obvious structure. Here as well, contrasting shapes remain very important. Expand the color scheme with violet, a color that makes a perfect combination with purple and red-purple. Purple with violet-blue and blue is a somewhat sombre and dark combination requiring complementary yellow or light red-purple; use light shades so the sombre impression disappears. Flowers that are truly blue, such as the blue poppy *Meconopsis betonicifolia*, do not combine well with purple.

Green and yellow-green flowers go marvelously well with purple. The yellow in the flowers makes the complementary purple more lively and the purple brings the yellow into the foreground, so an interesting overall picture is created. Green evokes its complementary color, red, so the purple seems redder. With light purple, grey-green leaves in particular are very attractive; they give a somewhat distinguished character to the purple. Dark, grey-purple leaves are also very attractive together with light shades of purple. But dark purple is a little sombre next to grey-purple leaves.

The complementary combinations purple/yellow and purple/orange are discussed in the chapter "Color Contrasts."

PURPLE IN LEAVES AND FRUIT

Many dark leaves are grey-purple in color, i.e., purple with some black mixed in. This color can be reproduced very well using purple and black watercolors. There are also leaves that are more grey-red or grey-orange. Hold a leaf up against the light to determine if purple, red, or orange is the dominant color. Colors frequently change however, since new leaves are often different in color. This makes it often difficult to determine the exact color.

Dark leaves are great for making combinations in a border. They can be used to insert obvious accents and they combine well with most colors. Some flowers are grey-purple; for example, those of the hollyhock and the smokeweed *Eupatorium maculatum* "Atropurpureum," a beautiful tall plant with dark grey-purple stems. For shrubs with dark leaves, choose from among several maples, such as *Acer palmatum* "Atropurpureum" and *Acer platanoides* "Crimson King," as well as *Berberis thunbergii* "Atropurpurea," the hazel *Corylus maxima* "Purpurea," the smoke tree *Cotinus coggygria* "Royal Purple," which also has grey-purple flowers and flower stalks, the well-known European beech *Fagus sylvatica* "Purpurea," the cherry plum *Prunus ceracifera* "Atropurpurea," with light red-purple flowers, and *Weigela florida* "Purpurea," with light red-purple flowers. There

Left
Dark, grey-purple leaves of the plantain *Plantago major* "Purpurea" intermingled with the orach *Atriplex hortensis* "Red Plume."

Right
This Japanese maple *Acer palmatum* "Dissectum Atropurpureum" retains its dark, grey-purple leaves all summer.

is a wide selection also among the perennials, including: *Acaena microphylla* "Copper Carpet"; carpet bugleweed *Ajuga reptans* "Atropurpurea" (violet flowers); the perennial virgin's-bower *Clematis recta* "Purpurea" (white flowers); spurge *Euphorbia amygdaloides* "Purpurea" (green flowers); fennel *Foeniculum vulgare* "Giant Bronze" (yellow flowers); alumroot *Heuchera micrantha* "Palace Purple" (white flowers); *Houttuynia cordata* (white flowers); *Ligularia dentata* "Desdemona" and "Othello" (orange flowers); *Lobelia fulgens* "Queen Victoria" (red flowers); the almost black *Ophiopogon planiscapus* "Ebony Night"; the ornamental grass *Panicum virgatum* "Rehbraun"; the wide plantain *Plantago major* "Purpurea" (green flowers); rhubarb *Rheum palmatum* "Atrosanguineum" (red-purple flowers); the medicinal plant sage *Salvia officinalis* "Tricolor," with leaves containing grey-green, white, and grey-purple specks (violet flowers); saxifrage *Saxifraga cortusifolia* "Rubrifolia," with the underside of the leaves a grey-purple color (white flowers); sedum *Sedum telephium* ssp. *maximum* (yellow flowers) and *Sedum* "Robustum" (red-purple flowers); four-leaf clover *Trifolium repens* "Pentaphyllum"; and violets *Viola labradorica* (violet flowers)

A well-known annual with grey-purple leaves is orach *Atriplex hortensis* "Red Plume." The cultivated annual castor-oil plant *Ricinus communis* "Gibsonii" has large, dark leaves. And from the herb garden comes the fragrant basil *Ocimum basilicum* "Dark Opal." The shrub *Callicarpa bodenieri* var. *giraldii* surprisingly follows up on its purple flowers with conspicuously purple-colored round little fruits. This shrub also has magnificent orange foliage in the fall. After producing green flowers with a blue nap, the *Decaisnea fargesii* yields grey-purple, pickle-shaped fruits that stay attached to the shrub for a long time.

BORDER IN WHITE, RED-PURPLE, PURPLE, AND VIOLET

This is a romantic border with flowers in soft colors, going from red-purple to violet and a few blue accents. The design is by the recently deceased Mrs. Canneman, who planted splendid gardens for the De Walenburg castle in Langbroek, Holland. The gardens can still be visited a few days each year. Mrs. Canneman used the colors white, red-purple, purple, purple-violet, and violet almost exclusively in her color combinations. She hardly used pure red or yellow at all. She used many foliage plants with grey leaves, such as large cotton thistle and artemisias.

In the original border, an oblong pond was located in the center with a colorful border on each side. You can see this design brought to life in the Model Gardens. In this book is just one of the borders with a dark green *Taxus* hedge along its edge. It has been trimmed to straight lines. The hedge is clipped and tapered in order to keep it nice and full. In between the plants and the hedge a narrow strip is kept clear so the *Taxus* gets enough light close to the ground as well. The conically trimmed white spruce trees are very striking. They stand like sentinels in the border.

This is a border for true plant-lovers, since it requires quite a lot of maintenance. The plants must be fertilized carefully and tied up, and the tussocks must be secured in their places. But, if cared for well, there is much to enjoy in this border. In April, the first flowers of *Arabis caucasica* "Rosea" appear. They are followed by summer phloxes, bellflowers, and many other beautiful flowers during the summer months. In October, colorful Michaelmas daisies complete the display.

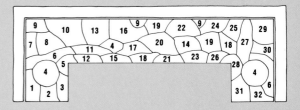

Design: Mrs. Canneman-Philipse/Modeste Herwig

Measurements: 38 × 12 ft. (11.5 × 3.5 m.)

Purple in Plant Names

atropurpureus—dark purple-red
purpurascens—in the process of becoming purple
purpuratus—with a purple haze
purpureomaculatus—with purple specks
purpureoroseus—purple-pink
purpureus (-a, -um)—purple-red

110

DESIGN AND LIST OF PLANTS

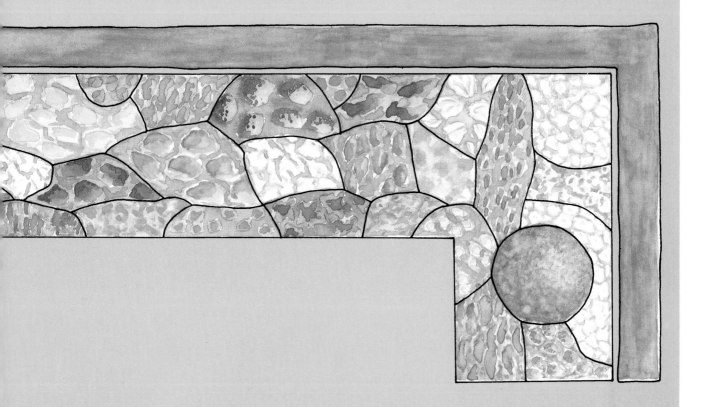

1 Self-heal, *Prunella grandiflora* "Loveliness"

2 Lamb's ear, *Stachys byzantina* "Silver Carpet"

3 Gypsohila, *Gypsohila* "Rosy Veil"

4 White spruce, *Picea glauca* "Conica"

5 Horned violet, *Viola cornuta* "Jersey Gem"

6 Rock cress, *Iberis sempervirens* "Snowflake"

7 Catmint, *Nepeta faassenii* "Six Hills Giant"

8 Common yarrow, *Achillea millefolium* "Red Beauty"

9 Cotton thistle, *Onopordum acanthium*

10 Larkspur, *Delphinium belladonna* "Lamartine"

11 Michaelmas daisy, *Aster dumosus* "Prof. Anton Kippenberg"

12 Carnation, *Dianthus plumarius* "Artis"

13 Michaelmas daisy, *Aster novi-belgii* "Crimson Brocade"

14 Masterwort, *Astrantia major* "Margery Fish"

15 Knotweed, *Polygonum affine* "Superbum"

16 Bellflower, *Campanula lactiflora* "Loddon Anna"

17 Summer phlox, *Phlox decussata* "The King"

18 Artemisia, *Artemisia ludoviciana* "Silver Queen"

19 Centranth, *Centranthus ruber*

20 Summer phlox, *Phlox decussata* "Amethyst"

21 Italian aster, *Aster amellus* "Rudolf Goethe"

22 Larkspur, *Delphinium belladonna* "Völkerfrieden"

23 Fleabane, *Erigeron* "Darkest of All"

24 Michaelmas daisy, *Aster novi-belgii* "Fellowship"

25 Royal lily, *Lilium regale*

26 Arabis, *Arabis caucasica* "Rosea"

27 Lavender, *Lavandula angustifolia* "Munstead"

28 Crane's-bill, *Geranium endressii* "Wargrave Pink"

29 Shrub rose, *Rosa* "Mme Plantier"

30 Clary, *Salvia sclarea*

31 Speedwell, *Veronica gentianoides*

32 Germander, *Teucrium marum*

PURPLE TABLE

NAME	COMMON NAME	BLOOM/ MONTHS	LIGHT	HEIGHT IN INCHES	TYPE	PLANTS PER YD²	NOTES
Acaena microphylla "Copper Carpet"		6–7	○	2–4	○	12	grey-purple leaves; red fruit
Acanthus mollis	Artist's acanthus	6–8	○	30–40	○	3	grey-green leaves
Acer palmatum "Atropurpureum"	Japanese maple	4–5	◐	to 16 ft	⊛		grey-purple leaves
Acer platanoides "Crimson King"	Norway maple	4	○ ◐	to 40 ft	⊛		grey-purple leaves
Achillea millefolium "Cerise Queen"	Common yarrow	6–8	○ ◐	20–30	○	7	
Alcea rosea nigra	Hollyhock	7–9	○	to 10 ft	⊙ ⊙	5–7	dark grey-purple
Anemone hupehensis "Praecox"	Japanese anemone	8–9	○ ◐	20–30	○	5–7	
Aster novi-belgii "Alice Haslam"	Michaelmas daisy	9–10	○	10–20	○	7	
Aster ericoides "Ruth McConnell"	Heath aster	9–10	○	20–30	○	7	
Aster lateriflorus horizontalis	Aster	9–10	○	40–50	○	5	
Aster novi-belgii "Fellowship"	Michaelmas daisy	9–10	○	50–60	○	5	butterfly plant
Astilbe arendsii "Amethyst"	Spiraea	7–8	○ ◐	20–30	○	5–7	
Astilbe chinensis "Superba"	Spiraea	8–9	○ ◐	4–10	○	7	
Atriplex hortensis "Red Plume"	Orach	7–9	○ ◐	30–40	⊙	7–9	grey-purple leaves
Berberis thunbergii "Atropurpurea"	Japanese barberry	5–6	○	to 7 ft	⊛	1	grey-purple leaves
Buddleia davidii "Border Beauty"	Summer lilac	7–9	○	to 10 ft	⊛		prune back in the spring
Callicarpa bodinieri var. *Giraldii*	Beauty berry	6–7	○ ◐	to 7 ft	⊛	1–2	purple fruit
Campanula glomerata	Clustered bellflower	6–8	○ ◐	20	○	7	
Centaurea bella	Knapweed	6–7	○	10	○	7–9	
Centaurea dealbata "Steenbergii"	Knapweed	7–8	○	20–30	○	5–7	
Chelone obliqua	Turtlehead	8–10	◐	30–50	○	7	
Clematis "Dr. Ruppel"		6–7	○ ◐	to 10 ft	⊛	1	climber
Clematis "Margaret Hunt"		6–9	○ ◐	to 10 ft	⊛	1	climber
Clematis alpina "Willy"	Virgin's bower	5	○ ◐	to 7 ft	⊛	1	climber
Clematis viticella	Virgin's bower	7–9	○ ◐	to 13 ft	⊛	1	climber
Cotinus coggygria "Royal Purple"	Smoke tree	6–7	○	to 10 ft	⊛	1	grey-purple leaves
Crocus tommasinianus	Crocus	2–3	○ ◐	2–4	⊛	20–25	light purple
Decaisnea fargesii	Delphinium	5–6	○	to 7 ft	⊛	1	grey-purple fruit
Delphinium "Astolat"		6–7	○	60–70	○	5–7	
Erigeron "Die Fee"		6–8	○	20–30	○	5–7	light purple
Erysimum "Bowles Mauve"	Wallflower	5–8	○	10–20	⊙	5–7	grey-green leaves
Eupatorium maculatum "Atropurpureum"	Smokeweed	8–9	○ ◐	40–60	○	2–3	butterfly plant
Fagus sylvatica "Purpurea Nana"	European beech	4–5	○ ◐	to 13 ft	⊛		remains small; grey-purple leaves
Galega officinalis	Goat's rue	7–8	○	40–60	○	1–2	
Geranium macrorrhizum "Czakor"	Cranesbill	6–7	○ ◐	10–20	○	5–7	
Geranium oxonianum "Claridge Druce"		6–7	○ ◐	10–20	○	5–7	
Geranium sanguineum "Max Frei"	Cranesbill	5–8	○ ◐	10	○	5–7	
Gypsophila paniculata "Rosy Veil"		7–8	○	30–40	○	5	
Heliotropium arborescens	Heliotrope	6–10	○	10–20	⊛	7–9	cultivated as an annual
Hemerocallis "Pardon Me"	Day lily	6–8	○ ◐	20–30	○	3–5	dark purple
Heuchera micrantha "Palace Purple"	Alumroot	5–6	○ ◐	10–20	○	7	grey-purple leaves
Hosta "Betsy King"	Hosta	7–8	○ ◐ ●	8–16	○	5	blooms abundantly
Lamium orvala		4–6	◐ ●	10–20	○	3–5	grey-purple flowers
Lathyrus odoratus "Elizabeth Taylor"	Sweet pea	6–10	○	to 10 ft	⊙	3–5	light purple; fragrant; climber
Limonium latifolium	Sea lavender	7–8	○	10–20	○	7	dry soil; dry flower
Lythrum virgatum "Rose Queen"	Loosestrife	7–8	○ ◐ ●	30–40	○	5	
Malva moschata "Rosea"	Muskmallow	6–8	○ ◐	20–30	○	5	light purple
Mentha longifolia "Buddleia"	Horsemint	7–8	○ ◐	20–30	○	5–7	
Monarda "Aquarius"	Bergamot	7–9	○ ◐	30–50	○	7	
Ocimum basilicum "Dark Opal"	Sweet basil	6–7	○	8–16	⊙	7–9	grey-purple leaves
Origanum "Herrenhausen"		8–10	○	10–20	○	7–9	butterfly plant
Penstemon "Sour Grapes"	Penstemon	7–9	○	16–24	○	7–9	not winter hardy
Penstemon hirsutus	Beard-tongue	5–7	○	16–24	○	7	sensitive to frost
Phlox arendsii "Hilda"	Phlox	5–6	◐	16–24	○	9–11	
Phlox carolina "Magnificence"	Thick-leaf phlox	6–8	○ ◐	20–30	○	9	
Phlox paniculata	Summer phlox	7–9	○ ◐	50–60	○	5–7	light purple
Phlox paniculata "Elizabeth Arden"	Summer phlox	7–9	○ ◐	50–60	○	5–7	
Phlox paniculata "Lilac Time"	Summer phlox	7–9	○ ◐	50–60	○	5–7	light purple

NAME	COMMON NAME	BLOOM/ MONTHS	LIGHT	HEIGHT IN INCHES	TYPE	PLANTS PER YD²	NOTES
Phlox paniculata "Wilhelm Kesselring"	Summer phlox	7–9	○ ◑	50–60	○	5–7	
Phlox subulata "Benita"	Summer phlox	4–5	○	2–4	○	9–11	
Phlox subulata "Temiskaming"	Summer phlox	4–5	○	2–4	○	9–11	
Physostegia virginiana "Bouquet Rose"	Obedience	7–9	○	30–40	○	7	light purple
Primula vialii	Primrose	6–7	◑	10–20	○	7–9	
Prunella grandiflora "Loveliness"	Self-heal	6–9	○ ◑	4–10	○	7–9	
Prunus cerasifera "Atropurpurea"	Cherry plum	3–4	○ ◑	to 26 ft	✳	1	grey-purple leaves
Rheum palmatum "Atrosanguineum"	Rhubarb	6	○ ◑	to 7 ft	○	1	grey-purple leaves
Rosa "Comtesse de Murinais"	Rose	6	○	to 7 ft	✿	1	
Rosa "Interlav (Lavender Dream)"	Rose	6–10	○	30–60	✿	1	
Rosa "Tuscany"	French rose	6–7	○	20–40	✿	1	
Salvia officinalis "Purpurascens"	Common sage	6–7	○	10–20	✿	7	grey-purple leaves
Saxifraga cortusifolia "Rubrifolia"	Saxifrage	10–11	◑ ⬤	10–12	○	9	grey-purple leaves
Stachys grandiflora	Nettle	7–8	○ ◑	10–20	○	7	
Syringa vulgaris "Andenken an Ludwig Späth"	Common lily	5–6	○ ◑	to 13 ft	✿	1	single flowers
Teucrium lucidum	Germander	6–8	○	8–16	✿	5–7	evergreen
Thalictrum aquilegifolium	Meadow rue	5–7	○ ◑	30–40	○	5–7	
Thymus serpyllum	Lemon thyme	7–9	○	2–4	○	7–9	ground cover
Trifolium repens "Pentaphyllum"	White clover	6–9	○ ◑	4–8	○	7–9	grey-purple leaves
Verbascum "Pink Domino"		6–8	○	30–40	⊙	5	light purple
Verbena hastata "Rosea"	Blue vervain	7–9	○	30–40	○	7	light red-purple
Veronica spicata "Erica"	Speedwell	6–8	○	16–24	○	7	
Viola cornuta "Anneke"	Horned violet	6–10	○ ◑	4–8	○	9–11	
Viola cornuta "Molly Sanderson"	Horned violet	6–10	○ ◑	4–8	○	9–11	dark purple

○ full sun; ◑ partial shade; ⬤ shade
○ perennial plant; ⊙ biennial; ○ annual; ⊛ bulb; ⊕ tuber; ✿ shrub; ✳ tree

The garden with pond in the Model Gardens designed by Mrs. Canneman. The border design in this chapter is based on this design.

VIOLET

Violet has the shortest wavelength of light that the human eye can perceive. Ultraviolet has an even shorter wavelength and cannot be perceived by human beings, though it can be perceived by many insects. Ultraviolet occurs frequently in petals, especially in the form of conspicuous honey guides that signal nectar to the pollinators. The various shades of violet are difficult to distinguish from each other and hard to remember.

The fragrant flower violet used to be very popular for the production of perfume. Violet is the color of the moon, the mysterious queen of the night, and also of Diana, the goddess of the moon. There is a line in Shakespeare's A *Winter's*

Tale that reads, "Violets dim, but sweeter than the lids of Juno's eyes." This probably refers to the violet-colored substance that women in ancient Greece applied to their eyelids.

In color theory, violet has a restful effect and controls irritability. It is an inspiring color associated with spiritual development.

Left
Lavender creates violet edges along this path to a mysterious door.

Top
The magnificent violet flowers of *Clematis* "Perle d'Azur" act as background to the Lutyens garden bench at Sissinghurst.

THE VIOLET GARDEN

There are quite a lot of plants with purple-violet, violet, and violet-blue flowers. Violet is located between purple and blue and also retains a minute amount of red. Since blue is an attractive color to most people, violet flowers, and certainly violet-blue flowers, are almost always categorized as blue. Even purple flowers are sometimes called blue.

Violet is a cool color that "recedes"; a small garden with lots of violet will therefore seem somewhat larger. In addition, it is a very quiet color that will never be too obtrusive in a small garden. In the shade, lighter shades of violet come across especially well at dusk.

This chapter's border design by Piet Oudolf, a well-known nurseryman and landscape gardener from Hummelo, the Netherlands, demonstrates that violet is very beautiful as the main color in a border. Next to violet and violet-blue, a few purple and blue flowers have also been used.

Left
A small area of a violet border with two kinds of crane's bill, the large *Geranium* "Johnson's Blue," and the much smaller *G. x cantabrigiense.*

Right
The dark violet irises make a good color combination with the white daisies. But it makes the violet look darker and this is why the color does not show up as well.

COMBINATIONS WITH VIOLET

Violet is an easy color for combinations because it actually matches all other colors. It is far enough away from orange and red and is still slightly related to purple and red-purple.

As is the case when combined with purple, white appears very harsh in combination with dark violet and makes this already dark color seem even darker. White looks better with the lighter shades; light violet flowers also look darker next to white, but with these, white serves to make their color stand out better. Cream-colored flowers also go well with violet. *Clematis recta*, for example, is very beautiful with violet larkspurs.

Violet looks very good next to yellow-green; this is a light color that looks cheerful next to violet, a dark color, thus creating an obvious light-dark contrast. Among too much green, dark violet loses some of its

visibility, especially when both colors have approximately the same degree of brightness. Violet stands out much better next to grey-green and blue-green leaves. A very mysterious effect may arise when this combination is used, as happened in my garden when the blue-green grass *Leymus arenarius* (formerly called *Elymus*), which tends to grow rampant, began to march toward the violet-blue *Clematis durandii*.

In the border design provided in this chapter, the color scheme purple, violet, and blue has been used. These are all cool colors, among which only purple has a somewhat warm nature. These colors are located in the same section of the color circle and, therefore, not much can go wrong. Alternating light and dark shades makes the overall picture more lively. A few yellow disks, as in the *Thalictrum*, provide a subtle complementary contrast.

The combination of violet with yellow, orange, or red will be discussed in the chapter "Color Contrasts," and the combination red-purple, purple, and violet was discussed in the previous chapter.

117

Top left
A beautiful combination of various shades of purple and violet at Sissinghurst.

Center left
The violet-blue virgin's-bower *Clematis x durandii* among the grey leaves of the willow *Salix lanata.*

Bottom left
A large double border in violet, red-purple, and white. Along the edges are violet catmint (*Nepeta x faassenii*) and white *Crambe cordifolia.*

Right
The violet-blue of the African lily (*Agapanthus*) recurs in the clary (*Salvia sclarea*).

Blue-violet is the color of the soul

Blue-violet turns the eternal cycle's wheel, forever on and on

as long as life enchants the soul

Herko Groot

A BORDER IN VIOLET

This border, specifically designed for this book by Piet Oudolf, is a real summer border. The plants require full sun and the soil must let water through easily. Violet is the main color in this border while, in addition, a few purple and blue flowers have been used.

The flowers of the carpet bugleweed "Catlin's Giant" already appear in April; in May, it is the turn of the mountain bluet, and there are also a few plants that flower in June. But it is only in July-August that the border reaches its exuberant high point, while it will still be very attractive in September. It contains many unusual and new plants that you will not come across everywhere. Abundantly flowering summer phloxes combine beautifully with plants that grow a lot more sparsely, such as the meadow rue *Thalictrum rochebrunianum*. More towards the front in the border are the unusual gentian *Gentiana asclepiadea* and the sea lavender from Russia. The exquisite, light violet-blue flowers of the crane's bill *Geranium pratense* "Mrs. Kendall Clark" form a regularly recurring color theme in the design. As a little something extra, the leaves of this plant will display magnificent orange-red colors in late summer. The *Lobelia* is not totally winter-hardy and must be carefully covered up when there is frost in winter.

For more color in spring, distribute some bulbs among the perennials. Use varieties of the *Scilla* to get shades of violet. But, since there is otherwise very little violet to be seen as yet, choose a totally different color—for example, the sunny yellow of cheerful daffodils. The leaves of the bulbs will subsequently disappear when the perennials start coming out.

The border consists of perennials, and it is clearly built up from low to high. Only the *Perovskia* is a low shrub that has to be trimmed close to the ground every spring. I recommend providing the tall plants with extra supports to keep them from falling over. For this purpose, use prunings of osier branches placed among the tussocks in May. The plants will quickly grow over the bare branches, which will later be used as perfect supports.

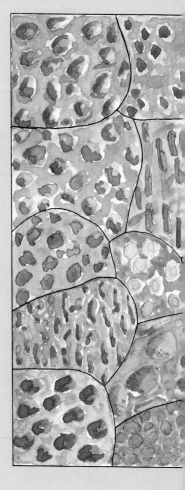

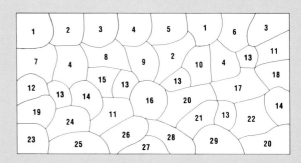

Design: Piet Oudolf. Measurements: 26 × 13 ft. (8 × 4 m.)

DESIGN AND LIST OF PLANTS

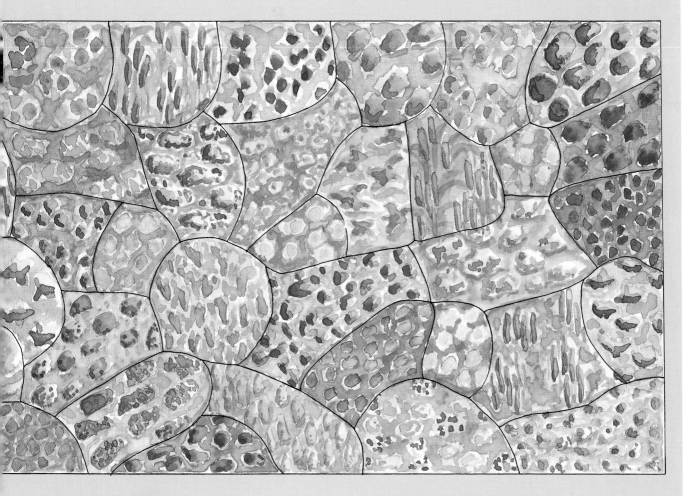

1 Summer phlox, *Phlox decussata*

2 Meadow rue, *Thalictrum rochebrunianum*

3 Bellflower, *Campanula lactiflora*

4 Speedwell, *Veronica virginicum*

5 Larkspur, *Delphinium* "Elmhimmel"

6 Small globe thistle, *Echinops ritro* "Veitch's Blue"

7 Bugloss, *Anchusa azurea* "Loddon Royalist"

8 Summer phlox, *Phlox decussata* "Blue Evening"

9 Blue wood aster, *Aster cordifolius*

10 Bergamot, *Monarda* "Elsie's Lavender"

11 Meadow rue, *Thalictrum delavayi*

12 Garden monkshood, *Aconitum carmichaelii*

13 Crane's bill, *Geranium pratense* "Mrs. Kendall Clark"

14 Eryngo, *Eryngium alpinum* "Blue Star"

15 Cupid's dart, *Catananche caerulea*

16 *Perovskia atriplicifolia* "Blue Spire"

17 *Kalimeris incisa*

18 Heath aster, *Aster ericoides* "Blue Star"

19 *Lobelia siphillitica*

20 Catmint, *Nepeta x faassenii* "Superba"

21 Gentian, *Gentiana asclepiadea*

22 Speedwell, *Veronica spicata* "Spitzentraum"

23 Mountain bluet, *Centaurea montana*

24 Sea lavender, *Limonium latifolium*

25 Horned violet, *Viola cornuta* "Boughton Blue"

26 Pot marjoram, *Origanum laevigatum* "Herrenhausen"

27 Carpet bugleweed, *Ajuga* "Catlin's Giant"

28 Sage, *Salvia x superba* "Blauhügel"

29 Balloon flower, *Platycodon grandiflorus* + bellflower *Campanula poscharskyana* "E.H. Frost"

VIOLET TABLE

NAME	COMMON NAME	BLOOM/ MONTHS	LIGHT	HEIGHT IN INCHES	TYPE	PLANTS PER YD²	NOTES
Aconitum carmichaelii	Monkshood	8–9	○ ◑	30–40	○	9	
Aconitum henryi "Spark"	Monkshood	6–8	○ ◑	30–50	○	9	
Aconitum napellus ssp. *pyramidale*	Garden monkshood	6–8	○ ◑	30–40	○	9	
Agastache foeniculum	Anise hyssop	7–8	○ ◑	30–40	○	7	bee plant
Allium aflatunense "Purple Sensation"	Flowering onion	5–6	○	30–40	ⓐ	12–16	
Allium unifolium	Flowering onion	5–6	○	6–12	ⓐ	12–16	light violet
Anemone blanda "Blue Shades"	Windflower	3–4	○ ◑	4–6	ⓑ	12–16	
Aquilegia vulgaris	Garden columbine	5–6	○ ◑	20–30	○	9	
Arabis caucasica "Rosea"	Wall rock cress	3–4	○	4–10	○	7	dry soil
Aster alpinus	Michaelmas daisy	5–6	○	8–16	○	7	
Aster amellus "Blue King"	Italian aster	8–9	○	20–30	○	7	
Aster amellus "Rudolf Goethe"	Italian aster	8–9	○	20–30	○	7	
Aster cordifolius "Photograph"	Blue wood aster	9–10	○	20–30	○	7	
Aster novi-belgii "Prof. Kippenburg"	Michaelmas daisy	9–10	○	50–60	○	7	
Aster ericoides "Blue Star"	Heath aster	9–10	○	20–30	○	7	
Aster frikartii "Jungfrau"	Michaelmas daisy	8–9	○	20–30	○	7	
Aster frikartii "Moench"	Michaelmas daisy	8–9	○	20–30	○	7	
Aster frikartii "Wonder of Stefa"	Michaelmas daisy	8–9	○	20–30	○	7	
Aster novi-belgii "Blue Bouquet"	Michaelmas daisy	9–10	○	50–60	○	5	butterfly plant
Aster novi-belgii "Climax"	Michaelmas daisy	9–10	○	50–60	○	5	butterfly plant
Aster "Lady in Blue"	Michaelmas daisy	9–10	○	50–60	○	5	butterfly plant
Aster novi-belgii "Little Boy Blue"	Michaelmas daisy	9–10	○	30–40	○	7	butterfly plant
Aster tongolensis "Berggarten"	Michaelmas daisy	5–6	○ ◑	10–20	○	7	
Baptisia australis	Blue false indigo	7–8	○	30–40	○	3	grey-green leaves
Brachycome iberidifolia "Blue Splendour"	Swan River daisy	7–9	○	6–12	⊙	7	
Calamintha nepeta	Calamint	7–10	○	8–16	○	7–9	
Camassia cusickii	Camass	5–6	○ ◑	20–30	ⓐ	5–7	light violet-blue
Campanula burghaltii	Bellflower	6–7	○ ◑	10–20	○	5–7	
Campanula carpatica "Blaue Clips"	Tussock bellflower	6–8	○ ◑	4–10	○	7–9	light violet-blue
Campanula carpatica "Blue Moonlight"	Tussock bellflower	6–8	○ ◑	4–10	○	7–9	light violet-blue
Campanula garganica "Major"	Bellflower	5–6	○ ◑	4	○	7–9	
Campanula lactiflora	Bellflower	6–8	○ ◑	30–40	○	7	
Campanula lactiflora "Pouffe"	Bellflower	6–8	○ ◑	12	○	7	
Campanula latifolia "Macrantha"	Bellflower	6–7	○ ◑	30–40	○	5–7	
Campanula porteschlagiana	Bellflower	6–7	○ ◑	4	○	7–9	
Campanula poscharskyana "E.H. Frost"	Bellflower	6–9	○ ◑	4	○	7–9	
Campanula rotundifolia	Bluebell	5–10	○ ◑	4–8	○	9–11	
Caryopteris clandonensis "Heavenly Blue"	Bluebeard	8–9	○	30–40	ⓦ	1–2	sensitive to frost
Catananche caerulea	Cupid's-dart	6–9	○	20–30	○	7	dried flower
Centaurea montana	Mountain bluet	5–8	○ ◑	10–20	○	5–7	
Clematis jackmanii "Gypsy Queen"	Virgin's bower	7–9	○ ◑	to 10 ft	ⓦ	1	climber
Clematis "Perle d'Azur"		7–8	○ ◑	to 10 ft	ⓦ	1	climber
Clematis integrifolia	Virgin's bower	6–7	○ ◑	30	○	1–2	wilted plant
Clematis macropetala "Markham's Pink"	Virgin's bower	5–6	○ ◑	to 10 ft	ⓦ	1	climber; light violet
Clerodendrum trichotomum	Glory-bower	8–9	○	to 16 ft	ⓦ ✳		violet berries
Convolvulus sabatius		6–9	○	10–20	○	3–5	not winter hardy
Delphinium "Berghimmel"	Delphinium	6–7	○	60–70	○	5–7	light violet-blue
Delphinium "Elmfreude"	Delphinium	6–7	○	60–70	○	5–7	white disk
Delphinium "Elmhimmel"	Delphinium	6–7	○	60–70	○	5–7	
Delphinium "Ouvertüre"	Delphinium	6–7	○	60–70	○	5–7	
Echinops ritro "Veitch's Blue"	Small globe thistle	7–9	○	40–50	○	3–5	grey-green leaves, bee plant
Erigeron "Darkest of All"		6–8	○	20–30	○	5–7	
Eryngium alpinum "Blue Star"	Eryngo	7–8	○	20–30	○	7	
Eryngium planum	Eryngo	7–8	○	30–40	○	7	
Gentiana triflora	Gentian	8–9	○ ◑	20–30	○	7	
Geranium pratense "Mrs. Kendall Clark"	Cranesbill	6–8	○ ◑	10–20	○	5–7	light violet-blue
Geranium renardii	Cranesbill	6	○ ◑	10	○	5–7	grey-green leaves
Geranium sylvaticum "Mayflower"	Cranesbill	6–7	○ ◑	20–30	○	5–7	light violet

NAME	COMMON NAME	BLOOM/ MONTHS	LIGHT	HEIGHT IN INCHES	TYPE	PLANTS PER YD²	NOTES
Geranium wallichianum "Buxton's Variety"	Cranesbill	7–10	○ ◑	10–20	○	5–7	
Hibiscus syriacus "Coelestis"	Rose-of-Sharon	8–9	○	to 10 ft	shrub	1	not winter hardy
Hyacinthoides hispanica	Hyacinth	5–6	○ ◑	10–20	bulb	12–15	
Hydrangea macrophylla "Mariesii Perfecta"	French hydrangea	7	○ ◑	to 7 ft	shrub	1	
Ipheion uniflorum	Spring starflower	4–5	○	4–8	bulb	20–25	light violet
Ipomoea tricolor "Praecox"	Morning-glory	8–9	○	to 10 ft	annual	1–2	climber
Iris germanica "Ambassadeur"	Fleur-de-lis	6	○	30–40	tuber	7	dry soil
Iris hoogiana	Fleur-de-lis	5–6	○ ◑	20	bulb	9–11	
Iris sibirica "Summer Sky"	Siberian iris	6	○ ◑	30–40	○	7	violet and yellow
Kalimeris incisa		6–9	○ ◑	30–40	○	5	
Lathyrus odoratus "Noel Sutton"	Sweet pea	6–10	○	to 10 ft	annual	3–5	climber
Lavandula angustifolia "Munstead"	English lavender	6–7	○	10–20	shrub	5–7	grey-green leaves; butterfly plant
Linaria purpurea	Spurred snapdragon	5–9	○	30–40	○	7	
Lupinus "The Governor"	Lupine	6–7	○ ◑	30–40	○	3	
Malva sylvestris "Primley Blue"	High mallow	6–9	○	8–16	biennial	3–5	light violet-blue
Mertensia echioides	Bluebells	5–6	○	16	○	7	
Mertensia virginica	Virginia bluebells	4–5	◑ ●	16–24	○	7	
Monarda "Elsie's Lavender"		7–9	○ ◑	30–40	○	7	light violet
Nepeta faassenii "Six Hills Giant"	Catmint	6–9	○ ◑	10–20	○	7	grey-green leaves
Nepeta nervosa	Catmint	7–9	○	10–12	○	7–9	
Nepeta sibirica	Siberian catmint	7–8	○ ◑	30–40	○	7	
Perovskia atriplicifolia "Blue Spire"		8–9	○	20–30	shrub	3	grey-green leaves
Phacelia tanacetifolia		6–8	○ ◑	20–30	annual	7–9	bee plant
Phlox divaricata "Clouds of Perfume"	Wild sweet William	5–6	◑	10–20	○	9–11	light violet-blue
Phlox paniculata "Amethyst"	Summer phlox	7–9	○ ◑	50–60	○	5–7	
Phlox paniculata "Blue Evening"	Summer phlox	7–9	○ ◑	50–60	○	5–7	
Phlox paniculata "Lavendelwolke"	Summer phlox	7–9	○ ◑	50–60	○	5–7	
Phlox paniculata "The King"	Summer phlox	7–9	○ ◑	50–60	○	5–7	
Platycodon grandiflorus	Balloon flower	7–8	○ ◑	20–30	○	9	
Polemonium caeruleum "Lambrook Mauve"	Jacob's-ladder	5–7	◑	20	○	7	light violet
Polemonium jacobaea "Richardsonii"	Jacob's-ladder	5–6	○ ◑	20–30	○	7	
Primula denticulata	Primrose	3–4	○ ◑	8–12	○	9	
Pulmonaria saccharata "Cambridge Blue"	Bethlehem sage	4–5	◑ ●	10	○	7–9	light violet-blue
Salvia farinacea	Mealy-cup	6–10	○	20–30	○	7–9	cultivated as an annual
Salvia nemorosa "Amethyst"	Sage	6–8	○ ◑	20–30	○	7	
Salvia nemorosa "Blauhuegel"	Sage	6–8	○ ◑	16–24	○	7	
Salvia nemorosa "May Night"	Sage	6–8	○ ◑	20–30	○	7	
Salvia nemorosa "Tänzerin"	Sage	6–8	○ ◑	20–30	○	7	
Salvia sclarea	Cleary	6–7	○	50–60	biennial	3	light violet-blue and white
Salvia verticillata "Purple Rain"	Lilac sage	6–9	○ ◑	16–24	○	5–7	
Salvia viridis "Blue Bird"	Sage	6–9	○ ◑	10–20	biennial	7–9	
Scabiosa caucasica "Clive Greaves"	Pincushion flower	7–9	○ ◑	30–40	○	5–7	
Scabiosa lucida	Pincushion flower	6–8	○	20–30	○	5–7	butterfly plant
Scutellaria incana	Skullcap	8–9	○	20–30	○	7	grey-green leaves
Silene coeli-rosa "Blue Pearl"		7–8	○	10–20	biennial	7–9	
Thalictrum delavayi	Meadow rue	7–8	○ ◑	60–70	○	5	
Thalictrum rochebrunianum	Meadow rue	7–8	○ ◑	60–80	○	3	
Verbena bonariensis	Vervain	7–10	○	50–60	○	7	Sensitive to frost; butterfly plant
Verbena hastata	Blue vervain	7–9	○	30–40	○	7	
Verbena rigida	Vervain	6–10	○	10–20	biennial	9–11	light violet
Veronica filiformis	Speedwell	4–6	○ ◑	1–2	○	7	ground cover
Veronica longifolia "Blauriesin"	Speedwell	7–9	○ ◑	30–40	○	5–7	
Veronica spicata "Spitzentraum"	Speedwell	6–8	○	16–24	○	7	grey-green leaves
Veronica virginica	Bowman's-root	7–8	○	50–70	○	5	
Veronica virginica "Fascination"	Bowman's-root	7–8	○	50–70	○	5	stem with band-shaped enlargement
Vinca minor	Common periwinkle	4–6	○ ◑ ●	6–8	shrub	5–7	evergreen ground cover
Viola cornuta	Horned violet	6–10	○ ◑	4–8	○	9–11	
Viola cornuta "Amethyst"	Horned violet	6–10	○ ◑	4–8	○	9–11	
Viola labradorica	Labrador violet	5	◑ ●	4–6	○	9–11	grey-green leaves
Viola odorata	Sweet violet	3–4	◑ ●	4–6	○	9–11	fragrant; ground cover

○ full sun; ◑ partial shade; ● shade
○ perennial plant; ⊙ biennial; ⊘ annual; ⊛ bulb; ⊕ tuber; ⊛ shrub; ⊕ tree

BLUE

Left
A refreshing
combination
of the white
bellflower and
violet-blue
larkspurs.

Flowers that
are any bluer
than this blue
poppy (*Me-
conopsis be-
tonicifolia*)
will be diffi-
cult to find.

Blue is a very attractive, magical color that is associated with the sky, the sea, and magnificent vistas. Picasso considered blue "the best of all colors." There is even an entire book in Dutch devoted to blue flowers, *Blauwe bloemen* (Blue Flowers). Our eyes are very sensitive to blue and we can distinguish many different shades of blue.

The unreachable blue of the heavens symbolizes infinity, the beyond, and also loyalty. Blue is the color of the mantle of Mary and is the color of serenity and sincerity.

Exceptionally honest and sincere people may be referred to as "true blue." Blue is also a cold color, the color of coolness and darkness. It is the color of regret, disappointment, deceit, and passivity. "Having the blues" means being depressed or melancholy.

People's fondness for blue goes back thousands of years, but there are not many natural blue dyes. The blue pigment ultramarine was formerly made from ground blue lapis lazuli. In Ancient Egypt, it was used as precious eye shadow; in the Middle Ages, the illuminators of books used it to make blue paint.

The well-known indigo, a plant that is easy to grow, has for a very long time now served as blue dye for work clothes and denim. Those of us who are fond of blue will be classified by the color therapies as people who are meticulous, stable, and satisfied with what they have achieved. Blue is a passive color that makes people feel calm and relaxed, but too much blue has an inhibiting effect and impedes growth. Plants that are exposed to blue light experience serious disturbances of their growth patterns. Blue light causes fatigue and depression, and it slows down the pulse rate; hence it gives us the blues.

THE BLUE GARDEN

Unfortunately, not many flowers are truly blue; most flowers that are called blue are violet or purple. The famous blue rose really does not exist! In the Blue Table is a reasonable selection of blue flowers, definitely enough to make a blue garden. The Blue Table also includes flowers that are violet-blue, which borders on blue. Unfortunately, blue flowers do not show up well in photographs, so look at the living flowers to experience the charm of this splendid color. Blue is very restful to the eyes and makes a garden look bigger. It is reminiscent of the misty blue of a panoramic view, when everything that is far away is seen in a blue haze as a result of the diffusion of light in the atmosphere. However, a garden with only blue flowers is a little sombre. Dark blue especially does not show up well next to green. In addition, blue looks more purple due to the simultaneous contrast; green evokes red, its complementary color, and the red mixes with the blue.

In designing a blue garden, it is better not to be too inflexible about the color blue but rather to mix a little of another color in with the blue. Gertrude Jekyll, for example, designed a blue garden with pure blue, white, blue-green leaves, and some soft yellow. Some of the plants she used were larkspurs, *Salvia patens*, bugloss (*Anchusa*), Madonna lilies, the greyish eryngo *Eryngium giganteum*, and the soft yellow meadow rue *Thalictrum flavum*.

Soft yellow is a very appropriate color for making the slightly sombre color blue more lively. It creates a color-against-color contrast and a simultaneous contrast that makes the blue seem somewhat more purple. On a small scale, yellow disks and yellow stamens have the same effect.

The lighter shades of red-purple also look beautiful together with violet-blue and blue; they make a blue garden complete. The border design for this chapter is an example of this. Variegated leaves also look very refreshing with blue. A really beautiful example is the *Brunnera macrophylla* "Variegata," a plant with green-and-white-variegated leaves and blue flowers that is similar to the forget-me-not.

The bright blue of the beautiful blue poppy, *Meconopsis betonicifolia*, is very striking in a garden. Darker blue is less conspicuous and looks a little sombre, especially from a distance. Light blue, true baby blue, comes across as a lovely color and shows its true nature especially well in the shade; exposed to full sunlight, this color easily becomes too pale.

Top left
Caryopteris x
clandonensis
"Heavenly
Blue" is visited
by lots of bees.

Bottom left
Blue and
white are
colors selected
for this border
at Hidcote
Manor.

Top right
A blue border
with mountain
bluet, catmint,
crane's bill,
and light blue
irises. The red-
purple roses
make the dark
blue somewhat
more lively.

Bottom right
Dark blue
combines well
with light yel-
low and with
red-purple in
the blue bor-
der at the
Priona Gar-
dens.

**Blue arches
the heavenly
vault**

**Blue is the
color of love-
liness**

**Blue speaks
of battles
won**

**Blue brings
us from time
to eternity.**

Herko Groot

Top left
The red-purple rose "Raubritter" and the light violet-blue *Malva sylvestris* "Primley Blue" are in the blue border.

Bottom left
Unusual-looking bright blue garden furniture. In the background is red-purple indigo, also a shrub used in the blue border.

Top right
Green and violet-blue are an extremely good combination, as shown here by the green inflorescences of the *Veratrum album* and the large bells of the bellflower.

Bottom right
In the blue border, this exquisite combination is created with the red-purple peony "Sarah Bernhardt" and violet-blue larkspurs.

> The bluebell, with its spotless azure color, does not want to be worn by anyone other than those who are sincere.
>
> **William Brown**

COMBINATIONS WITH BLUE

True blue is not an easy color to make combinations with. The neutral color white looks very refreshing next to blue; creamy white also goes well with blue. When using dark blue, select greyish white, for example the loosestrife *Lysimachia ephemerum*, in order to avoid making the contrast too great.

As indicated above, blue and yellow make a perfect match; this combination is discussed in the last chapter. Do not use pure blue next to violet and purple; it definitely does not look good; it appears dull and seems to have lost all its expressiveness. Red-purple makes blue perk up enormously; the lighter shades especially are very subtle. In the border design included with this chapter, red-purple complements the blue beautifully. Some blue flowers fade to light red-purple with time, for example lungwort (*Pulmonaria*), and marvelous combinations are created. This discoloration has to do with processes in the plant that involve changes in acidity. Light green and yellow-green look marvelous next to blue and make this color more lively. Green does make blue seem more violet since green evokes a complementary red afterimage that mixes with blue, causing the blue to tend toward violet. Grey-green leaves are somewhat boring next to blue, but they can look attractive next to violet-blue.

Brown (grey-orange) shades look beautiful next to blue, their complementary color. For this combination, use terra-cotta materials or bricks. In the fall, leaves in this color are found in abundance.

The combinations of blue with its complementary orange and with red can be found in the chapter "Color Contrasts."

Blue in Plant Names

azureus (-a, -um)—azure or sky-blue
caeruleus—dark blue
cyanus—dark blue
glaucus—blue-green

A BLUE BORDER WITH RED-PURPLE ACCENTS

This L-shaped border uses plants with blue flowers interspersed with red-purple flowers used as accents. The red-purple is particularly noticeable. It accentuates the blue and makes the overall image much more cheerful than if only blue had been used. An unusual feature in this garden is the pergola, which offers support to climbers and creates a vertical element in the border. The pergola may be a simple wooden structure made of three square standards and four horizontal boards stained a dark color. The border must be placed in a rather sunny location, and the soil definitely must not be too wet. The true blue color is provided by such flowers as the bugloss, speedwell, and larkspurs. A number of violet-blue flowers have also been used. Together with the red-purple ones, light blue flowers give an impression of loveliness and ensure that the overall picture does not become too dark. For example, the light red-purple flowers of the rose "Raubritter," which grow in abundance, make a marvelous combination with the subtle light blue flowers of *Scabiosa caucasica* "Clive Greaves."

The periods when the plants in this border flower range from May to some time in October, so something is always going on. To see blue in the garden even earlier, plant some bulbs of the pure blue *Scilla sibirica* among the perennials. Very beautiful as well are the light blue flowers of the *Camassia cusickii*, which appear in April–May. Annuals can add even more blue to the border. The woodruff (*Asperula orientalis*) has a soft blue color. The viper's bugloss *Echium plantagineum* "Blue Bedder" displays various shades of blue and has red-purple buds. And blue forget-me-nots look marvelous as an edge along the border. The shrubs *Caryopteris* and *Indigofera* are sensitive to frost and may be affected if the winter is severe. However, they always bud again in the spring and they flower on old wood. To give them some help, throw a solid layer of leaves over the shrubs. *Clematis jouiniana* "Mrs. Robert Brydon" is not a true climber and must be tied onto the pergola with care. This shrub must be cut back considerably every spring, so it will keep its compact shape. The other two climbers, *Wisteria floribunda* and *Clematis alpina*, must be tied as well; they may also be cut back a little immediately after they stop flowering.

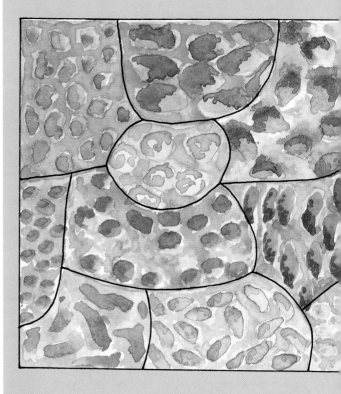

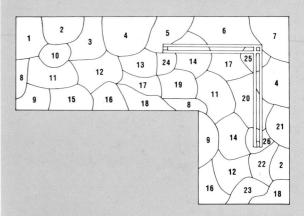

1 *Caryopteris x clandonensis* "Heavenly Blue"

2 Heath aster, *Aster ericoides* "Erlkönig"

3 Larkspur, *Delphinium* belladonna "Völkerfrieden"

4 Rose, *Rosa* "Raubritter"

5 Eryngo, *Eryngium alpinum* "Blue Star"

6 Indigo, *Indigofera amblyantha*

7 Virgin's-bower, *Clematis bonstedtii* "Crépuscule"

DESIGN AND LIST OF PLANTS

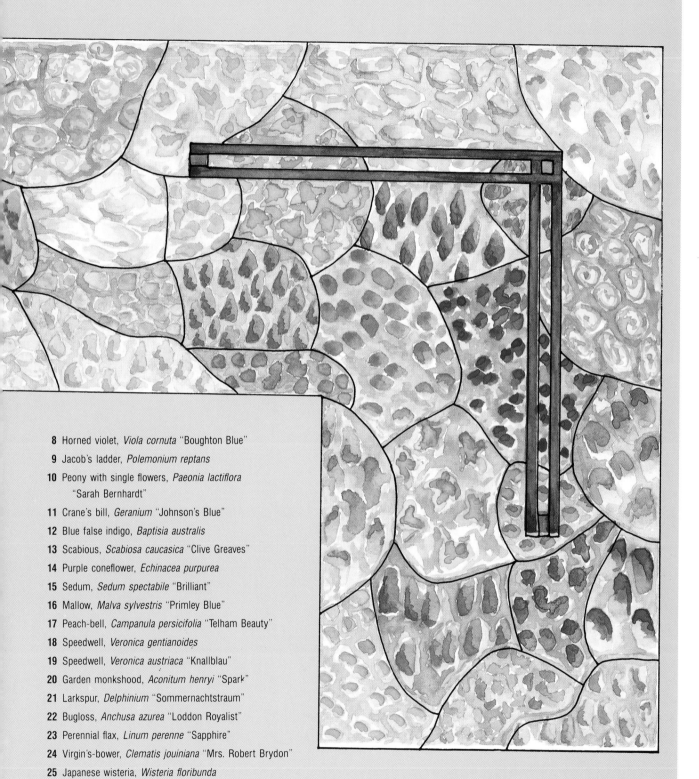

8 Horned violet, *Viola cornuta* "Boughton Blue"

9 Jacob's ladder, *Polemonium reptans*

10 Peony with single flowers, *Paeonia lactiflora* "Sarah Bernhardt"

11 Crane's bill, *Geranium* "Johnson's Blue"

12 Blue false indigo, *Baptisia australis*

13 Scabious, *Scabiosa caucasica* "Clive Greaves"

14 Purple coneflower, *Echinacea purpurea*

15 Sedum, *Sedum spectabile* "Brilliant"

16 Mallow, *Malva sylvestris* "Primley Blue"

17 Peach-bell, *Campanula persicifolia* "Telham Beauty"

18 Speedwell, *Veronica gentianoides*

19 Speedwell, *Veronica austriaca* "Knallblau"

20 Garden monkshood, *Aconitum henryi* "Spark"

21 Larkspur, *Delphinium* "Sommernachtstraum"

22 Bugloss, *Anchusa azurea* "Loddon Royalist"

23 Perennial flax, *Linum perenne* "Sapphire"

24 Virgin's-bower, *Clematis jouiniana* "Mrs. Robert Brydon"

25 Japanese wisteria, *Wisteria floribunda*

26 Virgin's-bower, *Clematis alpina* "Pamela Jackman"

Design: Modeste Herwig. Measurements: 30 × 20 ft. (9 × 6 m.)

BLUE TABLE

NAME	COMMON NAME	BLOOM/ MONTHS	LIGHT	HEIGHT IN INCHES	TYPE	PLANTS PER YD²	NOTES
Aconitum cammarum "Bicolor"	Monkshood	7–8	○ ◐	40–50	○	9	white with violet-blue
Agapanthus praecox	African lily	7–8	○	20–30	○	5	not winter hardy
Ajuga reptans "Atropurpurea"	Carpet bugleweed	5–6	◐ ●	6–8	○	9–11	grey-purple leaves
Ajuga reptans "Catlin's Giant"	Carpet bugleweed	5–6	○ ◐	10	○	9	large variety
Allium caeruleum	Flowering onion	6–7	○	20–30	⊚	12–16	
Anagallis monelli	Pimpernel	6–8	○	10–20	○	9–11	
Anchusa azurea "Loddon Royalist"	Bugloss	6–7	○	30–40	○	5–7	
Asperula orientalis	Woodruff	7–9	○ ◐	4–10	⊙	7–9	light violet-blue
Aster ericoides "Erlkönig"	Heath aster	9–10	○	20–30	○	7	
Berberis julianae	Wintergreen barberry	5–7	○ ◐	to 7 ft	⊛	1	blue berries
Borago officinalis	Talewort	6–9	○ ◐	20–30	⊙	5–7	
Borago pygmaea	Talewort	6–9	○ ◐	20–40	○	7	
Brunnera macrophylla		4–5	◐	10–20	○	5–7	beautiful leaves
Camassia quamash	Quamash	5–6	○ ◐	20–30	⊚	5–7	light blue
Campanula persicifolia "Telham Beauty"	Peach-bells	6–7	○ ◐	20–30	○	7	
Centaurea cyanus	Cornflower	5–7	○	30–40	⊙	7–9	
Ceratostigma plumbaginoides		9–10	○	10–20	○ ⊛	7	needs a protected location
Clematis "President"	Virgin's bower	5–9	○ ◐	to 10 ft	⊛	1	climber
Clematis alpina "Pamela Jackman"	Virgin's bower	5	○ ◐	to 7 ft	⊛	1	climber
Clematis bonstedtii "Crépuscule"	Virgin's bower	8–9	○ ◐	60–80	⊛	1	wilted plant
Clematis durandii	Virgin's bower	6–9	○ ◐	to 5 ft	⊛	1–2	
Clematis jouiniana "Mrs. Robert Brydon"	Virgin's bower	8–9	○ ◐	to 13 ft	⊛	1	tie up; prune back in fall
Commelina tuberosa	Dayflower	8–10	○	10–20	○	5–7	not winter hardy
Cornus amomum "Blue Cloud"	Silky dogwood	5–6	○ ◐	to 10 ft	⊛	1	blue berries
Cynoglossum amabile	Chinese forget-me-not	7–8	○ ◐	10–20	⊙	7–9	
Delphinium "Gletscherwasser"	Larkspur	6–7	○	60–70	○	5–7	light violet-blue
Delphinium "Sommernachtstraum"	Larkspur	6–7	○	60–70	○	5–7	
Delphinium belladonna "Lamartine"	Larkspur	6–7	○	50–60	○	5–7	
Delphinium belladonna "Völkerfrieden"	Larkspur	6–7	○	50–60	○	5–7	
Echinops banniaticus "Taplow Blue"		7–8	○	40–50	○	3–5	grey-green leaves; bee plant
Echium plantagineum "Blue Bedder"	Viper's bugloss	6–8	○	10–20	⊙	7–9	
Felicia amelloides	Blue daisy	6–10	○	16–24	○	5–7	not winter hardy
Gentiana asclepiadea	Gentian	8–9	○ ◐	20–30	○	7	
Gentiana sino-ornata	Gentian	9–10	○ ◐	4–6	○	7–9	acidic, damp soil
Geranium "Johnson's Blue"	Geranium	6–7	○ ◐	10–20	○	5–7	
Houstonia caerulea "Millard"	Bluets	4–6	◐	2	○	12–15	damp soil; not easy
Iris reticulata "Harmony"	Fleur-de-lis	3	○ ◐	6	⊚	12–15	
Iris sibirica "Silver Edge"	Siberian iris	6	○ ◐	30–40	○	7	violet-blue with white edges
Jasione "Blue Light"		7–8	○ ◐	8–12	○	9–11	
Linum perenne "Saphir"	Perennial flax	6–8	○	16–24	○	7	
Lobelia erinus "Cambridge Blue"	Edging lobelia	5–9	○	8–12	⊙	7–9	light violet-blue
Lobelia gerardii "Vedrariensis"		7–8	○	40–50	○	7	sensitive to frost
Lobelia siphilitica	Great lobelia	7–8	○	30–40	○	7	sensitive to frost
Mahonia aquifolium	Oregon grape	4–5	◐ ●	40–50	⊛	1	blue berries
Meconopsis betonicifolia	Blue poppy	6–7	◐	30–40	○	5–7	acidic, humus-rich soil
Muscari armeniacum	Grape hyacinth	4	○	6–10	⊚	20–25	
Myosotis alpestris	Forget-me-not	5–7	○ ◐	6–10	⊙	7–9	
Nemophila menziesii	Baby-blue-eyes	6–8	○	6–10	⊙	12–15	
Nigella damascena	Love-in-a-mist	6–9	○	10–20	⊙	7	
Omphalodes cappadocica	Navelwort	4–8	○ ◐	4–8	○	7	
Omphalodes verna	Creeping forget-me-not	4–5	○ ◐	4–8	○	7	
Phlox divaricata "Chattahoochee"	Wild sweet William	5–6	◐	10–20	○	9–11	sensitive to frost
Phlox divaricata "May Breeze"	Wild sweet William	5–6	◐	10–20	○	9–11	light violet
Phlox subulata "Alice Wilson"	Moss pink	4–5	○	2–4	○	9–11	
Polemonium reptans	Jacob's-ladder	5–6	○ ◐	16–24	○	7	
Pulmonaria angustifolia "Blaues Meer"	Lungwort	4–5	◐ ●	10	○	7–9	
Puschkinia scilloides		4–5	○ ◐	6	⊚	20–25	white with blue stripes
Salvia patens	Gentian sage	6–9	○	20–30	○	5–7	not winter hardy

NAME	COMMON NAME	BLOOM/ MONTHS	LIGHT	HEIGHT IN INCHES	TYPE	PLANTS PER YD²	NOTES
Salvia patens "Cambridge Blue"	Gentian sage	6–9	○	20–30	Ⓞ	5–7	not winter hardy; light blue
Scilla amethystina	Squill	5–6	○ ◑	8–10	ⓐ	12–15	
Scilla mischtschenkoana	Siberian sage	3–4	○	4–6	ⓐ	15–20	
Scilla sibirica	Siberian sage	3–4	○	4–6	ⓐ	15–20	
Symphytum azureum	Comfrey	4–5	○ ◑	10–20	Ⓞ	3–5	
Symphytum grandiflorum "Blaue Glocke"	Comfrey	4–5	◑ ●	6–10	Ⓞ	5–7	light blue
Veronica "Madame Mercier"	Speedwell	5–6	○ ◑	2–4	Ⓞ	9–11	ground cover
Veronica austriaca "Royal Blue"	Speedwell	6–7	○	8–16	Ⓞ	5–7	
Veronica gentianoides		5–6	○ ◑	12–16	Ⓞ	7	light violet-blue
Veronica incana		7–8	○	10–20	Ⓞ	7	grey-green leaves
Viola cornuta "Boughton Blue"	Horned violet	6–10	○ ◑	4–6	Ⓞ	9–11	light violet-blue
Wisteria floribunda	Japanese wisteria	5–6	○ ◑	to 26 ft	ⓦ	1	climber

○ full sun; ◑ partial shade; ● shade
Ⓞ perennial plant; ⊙ biennial; ○ annual; ⓐ bulb; ⓣ tuber; ⓦ shrub; ⊕ tree

BLUE BERRIES

Good additions to a blue garden are shrubs that produce violet-blue or blue berries. Unfortunately, dark berries are not very noticeable when they are too hidden among the green leaves. The wintergreen barberry *Berberis julianae*, which retains its leaves but is very winter-hardy, has small blue berries that are covered with hoarfrost and bears small yellow flowers in May. The glory-bower *Clerodendrum trichotomum* has white flowers in August followed by violet-blue berries that change to almost black. It is a shrub with a beautiful growth pattern for a protected spot. The silky dogwood *Cornus amomum* likes moist soil. This shrub has grey-purple branches and its foliage is a splendid orange-red in the fall; the "Blue Cloud" is a new variety, which is covered with blue fruit in late summer. The Oregon grape *Mahonia aquifolium* is beautiful already early in spring, with small, soft yellow flowers. During a large part of the summer, we can enjoy the small blue berries that grow in long clusters. The well-known blackthorn *Prunus spinosa* has vicious thorns but splendid white flowers in March and lots of dark blue fruit covered with bloom. There is also a variety with dark leaves that is called "Purpurea." The blueberry could have a spot in an ornamental garden as well. *Vaccinium angustifolium* "Top Hat" is a dwarf shrub with dark blue berries that also grows well in a pot. *Vaccinium corymbosum* grows to a height of 6½ ft. (2 m.) and bears numerous blue berries that get covered with white bloom. The fruit of both varieties is delicious. *Viburnum davidii*, a small arrowwood of up to 20 in. (50 cm), retains its leaves as well as its beautiful violet-blue berries all winter.

Plants with blue-green leaves are discussed in the chapter "Green" because the leaves are more green than blue.

In late summer, the Oregon grape bears beautiful bloom-covered blue berries that combine well with the red fall color of the shiny leaves.

GREEN

Left
Shape is very important in this mostly green border, where a little yellow and white are used.

A successful composition of leaves with different shapes near a small pond.

Green is the most important color in the garden because the colorful flowers are all inserted in their beds of green leaves. Green is the color of the fertile earth.

Green reminds us of streets planted with trees, cool and shady in summer, and of wide lawns surrounded by colorful borders. Light green is the color of spring, when all the buds burst open and the new, light green leaves appear.

Traditionally, green is the color of hope. Green is located between the stimulating color yellow and the quiet color blue. It is the color in the center of the spectrum.

And, as the color in the center, it is also the color of peace. In the Middle Ages, green was the color of joy and fertility and, therefore, the traditional color of the wedding gown. The "green wedding" referred to the festivities held when a marriage was contracted; and when a person was "green," it meant that he was in love. As the color of life, green is also the color of youth. This shows up in all sorts of well-known expressions, such as "greenhorn," meaning inexperienced; "he is as green as grass," meaning the person is still very naive; and the "green years," referring to youth.

Green is a quiet color that is not tiring to the eyes. Our eyes are most sensitive to yellow-green; all receptors are stimulated by it, so a sharp image is produced. As a restful color, green is often used for the interior of bedrooms.

Green too has its negative aspects; it is the color of jealousy and poison (poisonous green).

In color therapy, people with a preference for green are considered self-assured, modest types who love nature. The color green has a harmonizing, calming, and relaxing effect. The effect of green that tends towards blue is restful, while yellow-green is bracing.

THE GREEN GARDEN

In a green garden, flowers are of secondary importance while leaves are key. The many different shapes of leaves and the various shades of green make a green garden interesting. The attention is not distracted by vividly colored flowers and, as a result, all the beautiful leaves can be clearly distinguished. A few white and, of course, green flowers produce variety in a green garden, since the leaves convey a rather static image during a large part of the year. Evergreens especially can be a little boring because they show little change. In the Green Table is a selection of plants with green flowers and beautiful foliage. The list of the foliage can, of course, be expanded almost endlessly since there are so many green leaves!

Colors seem most intense when the surface is shiny, and this applies of course to green as well. Hence shiny leaves should definitely be used in the green garden. In addition, yellow-green and blue-green leaves can provide variety. Yellow-green is very cheerful and reminds us of spring. Blue-green is the coldest color in existence; too much of this color makes a garden appear very cool. Grey-green leaves, which have also been used extensively in the colorful border designs of the previous chapters, are indispensable in the green garden. The greyish color is the result of very fine hairs that protect the plant from dehydration. Plants with grey leaves are, in fact, generally indigenous to a rather dry and sunny climate. Only the life everlasting (*Anaphalis*) can be used in half shade, so this is truly a valuable plant. Variegated leaves are very exciting in a green garden and provide strong accents. Do use the accent carefully without overdoing it, so that the effect is not lost. Plants with white-variegated leaves can be found in the White Table and those with yellow-variegated leaves in the Yellow Table. Dark leaves are discussed in the chapter "Purple."

Take advantage of contrasting leaves in a green garden. Since there is only one color to look at, all attention goes to the shapes of the plants. The different shapes are reinforced by the contrasts of the shapes. For example, plant a *Hosta* with its large, almost round leaves next to gracefully feathered ferns, or plant the large rhubarb in front of a shrub with very small leaves. Large, clearly distinguishable shapes are provided by conifers that grow in the form of cones or spheres and by hedges trimmed to have straight lines as well as shrubs trimmed to various shapes. Some shrubs and trees have characteristic, cultivated varieties with unusual shapes; these may be drooping or very narrow shapes (often called *fastigiata*). Climbers can grow over a wall or a shed and, in so doing, make a boring surface part of the garden. With ground cover, you can create a restful background against which other plants stand out even more due to their shape or color.

In the garden, a lawn creates a large green horizontal surface that is easy to use as a quiet foreground in front of the colorful border. A light-dark pattern of lines is often created as a result of tracks left in the grass after mowing. If these lines are pointed in the lengthwise direction of the garden, the garden will seem larger. Diagonal lines can also be very exciting.

Extreme left
An attractive overall image is created by various shades of green in the herb garden at Sissinghurst. The thyme in the old fragrance bench infuses the clothing of all who sit on the bench with a delicious scent.

Left
Pots with trimmed *Buxus* have been incorporated into the green border. Various interesting shapes of leaves provide a beautiful composition.

Top right
The enormous leaves of the butterbur together with the leaves of the cow parsnip along the edge of a pond.

Bottom right
A garden can be interesting even without colorful flowers. Very important here are the shapes of the hedges trimmed to straight lines, the leaves of the *Hosta,* and the little trees pruned to spherical shapes on trunks.

The color of this pot makes a harmonious match with the plants it contains. Grey-green and yellow-green leaves, yellow-and-green-variegated leaves, and a few light yellow flowers make a splendid display.

Green is the color that proclaims youth

Green is the bud that bursts open

Green is the wood on which the sun shines

Green is the hope that never disappears

Herko Groot

COMBINATIONS WITH GREEN

When making color combinations in a garden, green serves as the basic structure since it is always present and complements the color scheme. And when the plants are past flowering, green becomes the main color in the garden. This is the reason why one of the criteria in the selection of plants is that they have beautiful leaves.

A selection can be made out of several different shades of green. Grey-green is a very neutral color that makes other colors stand out better. Soft pastels look especially attractive next to grey foliage plants, and grey-green should definitely not be omitted from a white garden. Grey-green itself is strongly influenced by adjacent colors precisely because it is so neutral. As a result of the simultaneous contrast, it acquires a haze of the complementary color of the neighboring plant. Hence it looks somewhat redder next to bright green leaves.

Yellow-green combines well with yellow flowers, but also with purple, violet, and blue. There are many plants with yellow-green leaves, such as, of course, the various *Hosta* varieties and pot marjoram and sage with their yellow leaves. But there are also all kinds of cultivated varieties of shrubs and conifers, such as maples, the honey locust (*Gleditsia*), locust (*Robinia*), the jasmine with yellow leaves, and many varieties of dwarf cypress (*Chamaecyparis*) and *Taxus*. There is a variety of the common privet that has yellow leaves, the *Ligustrum ovalifolium* "Aureum," a shrub that is easy to trim into various shapes.

Blue-green leaves go well with practically all colors; only bright blue is not very attractive in combination with blue-green. This color can be found in particular among the various varieties of *Hosta*, such as the large *H. sieboldiana* "Elegans" or the much smaller *H. tardiana* "Blue Moon," and among the ornamental grasses, such as the fescue (*Festuca*) and the beautiful couch grass *Agropyron pubiflorum*.

Green flowers go well with all colors. They are often somewhat yellow-green, and this goes especially well with yellow flowers and with violet and blue. Green flowers make a splendid color combination also with their complementary color red. The dark shades of red especially are made more lively by green. Green goes perfectly with white and this is the reason white can always be used in the green garden as well.

139

FOLIAGE PLANTS

Plants that are planted specifically for their beautiful leaves are called foliage plants. They can be used as solitary plants or as accents in an area filled with plants. Plants with very large leaves are immediately noticeable. The largest is the giant rhubarb *Gunnera tinctoria*, whose leaves can have a diameter of 6 ft. (2 m.)! However, this plant is not winter-hardy and must be covered carefully in winter. It likes moist soil rich in humus, for example, near a natural pond. But the plant is definitely not suitable for a small garden! The rhubarb *Rheum palmatum* bears somewhat smaller leaves. These are denticulate leaves whose underside is purplish. The leaves of the gigantic cow parsnip (*Heracleum mantegazzianum*) resemble the leaves of the rhubarb somewhat. Do be careful with this plant because touching the leaves may cause inflammation or leave ugly spots on the skin. The annual castor-oil plant (*Ricinus communis*) produces very large leaves in one year while reaching a height of about 6½ ft. (2 m.). The butterbur *Petasites hybridus* has somewhat smaller leaves that are still an impressive size.

The umbrella plant *Peltiphyllum peltatum* and the *Astilboides tabularis* have leaves that are somewhat smaller still and that are almost round; they also prefer slightly moist soil. The various varieties of *Rodgersia* have large leaves but are suitable for use in a somewhat smaller garden. The various *Hosta* varieties are very well known foliage plants and many of these are beautiful with their yellow-green, blue-green, or variegated leaves.

There are too many beautiful foliage plants to list, but I do want to mention the climbing birthwort (*Aristolochia*) with large heart-shaped leaves, the grey-leaved *Artemisias*, *Bergenia*, the grey-green cardoon (*Cynara cardunculus*), and English ivy (*Hedera*) with shiny leaves, the grey lamb's ears (*Stachys byzantina*), ferns, and *Veratrum* with large light green leaves. And don't forget the ornamental grasses, which make any area look airy with their elegant panicles.

Left
The broad leaves of the *Hosta sieboldiana* "Frances Williams" and the delicate leaves of the fern make an interesting contrast of shapes.

Top right
The pear *Pyrus salicifolia* "Pendula" is one of the most beautiful trees with grey leaves.

Bottom right
Already in summer, the virgin's-bower *Clematis alpina* "White Moth" is adorned with grows the greenish seed fluff. At the foot of the wall is beautiful loosestrife *Lysimachia ephemerum*.

GREEN SEEDS

Plants that have finished flowering often remain decorative-looking for a long time if they have beautiful seeds or seed vessels, which are often green. Much in demand for bouquets of dried flowers are the seed vessels of poppies. The opium poppy *Papaver somniferum* "Hen and Chickens" produces an additional circle of small vessels around the large seed vessel, very strange indeed. The annual love-in-a-mist produces delicate, globular seed vessels, which can often be seen in bouquets of dried flowers. The annual orach (*Atriplex hortensis*) and the *Thalictrum* varieties produce great quantities of small green seeds during late summer. A tree that bears lots of green seeds is the ash; the large clusters of green seeds are very conspicuous among the leaves, which have a much darker color. There are *Scabiosa* varieties that produce globe-shaped seed heads with a beautiful honeycomb pattern. The bulb *Eucomis bicolor* and several Christmas roses have green flowers as well as green seeds. There are *Clematis* varieties that produce fluffy seeds grouped in a kind of small wig. These are a very beautiful silver green on the *Clematis alpina* and *C. tangutica*. The *C. viticella* has sturdy seeds grouped in a very unusual manner to form a globule. And then of course the varieties of the parsley family, such as the large angelica, continue to look very decorative with their umbrellas full of green seeds even after they finish flowering.

PLANTS SUITABLE FOR HEDGES

Hedges are very important in a garden for dividing and setting off the available space. They form green walls for the different "rooms" in the garden. The yew, *Taxus baccata*, is a very dark green color and it remains green in winter and can easily be trimmed. It is one of the most beautiful hedges for use as background behind a colorful border and it also lends itself well to being trimmed into various shapes. Also the arborvitae (*Thuja*) and the dwarf cypress (*Chamaecyparis*) can be trimmed into beautiful winter hedges. Among the shrubs that retain their leaves, the following varieties are suitable for trimming: the well-known wintergreen barberry (*Berberis*), privet, holly, *Cotoneaster* and, for low hedges and all kinds of trimmed shapes, common boxwood (*Buxus*). Deciduous plants that are suitable for hedges include the beech (although the dry, brown leaves remain on the tree in winter), hornbeam, hawthorn, and field maple.

A GREEN BORDER

In this green border, which was designed specifically for this book by the landscape gardener Piet Oudolf, perennials are combined with various ornamental grasses. The perennials flower green or yellow-green and the ornamental grasses have brownish or silver-green panicles. A few plants with soft yellow flowers provide some variety.

In this border, shape is very important. The graceful, thin shapes of the ornamental grasses form contrasts with the sturdy shape of the tall angelica and the broad, flat flower shields of the common yarrow. Large bunches of the grasslike leaves of the day lily are combined with the delicate flowers of the masterwort and the elegant *Zigadenus elegans* ssp. *glaucus*. Beautifully shaped leaves can be seen on the Lady's-mantle, alumroot, sunflowers, and Christmas roses.

If you put off the "spring cleaning" to the spring, the border will be interesting in the winter as well. Especially when a little rime settles on the plants, the various grasses will be still very beautiful. The remaining parts of the angelica are also very decorative. In February, the Christmas rose already beings to put out its apple-green flowers, while the last flowers of the season are produced in October by the tall sunflower. Even more green is provided by the annual ornamental tobaccoes *Nicotiana* "Limegreen" and *N. langsdorffii*.

The black mullein is a biennial and the seeds must, therefore, be sowed every year again. The plant frequently sows itself, but you might as well help it a little, just to make sure. The Christmas rose *Helleborus argutifolius* must be covered in cases of severe frost, and the same applies to the *Zigadenus*.

Green in Plant Names

atrovirens—dark green
cinerea—ash grey (refers to grey-green leaves)
euchlora—with a beautiful green color
griseo-argenteo—silver grey
incana—grey
sempervirens—always green
virescens—light green
viridiflora—with green flowers
viridis—green

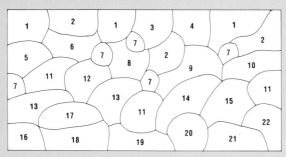

Design: Piet Oudolf. Measurements: 26 × 13 ft. (8 × 4 m.)

DESIGN AND LIST OF PLANTS

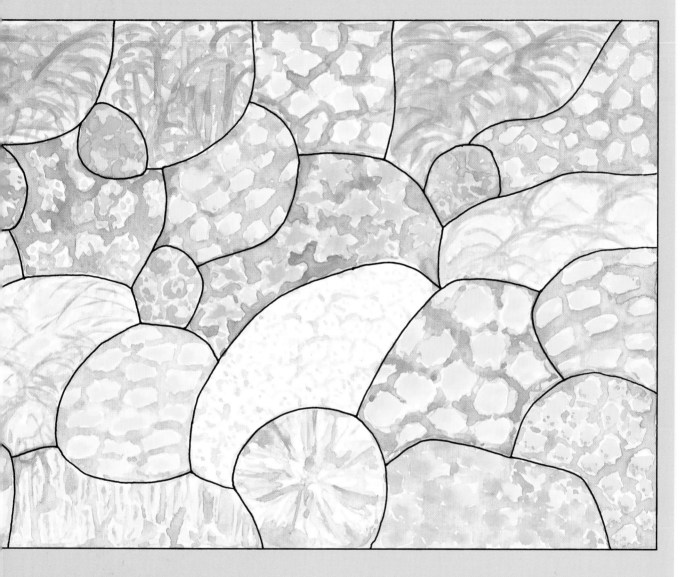

1 Sunflower, *Helianthus salicifolius*

2 Meadow rue, *Thalictrum flavum glaucum*

3 Eulalia, *Miscanthus sinensis* "Undine"

4 Giant scabious, *Cephalaria gigantea*

5 Bent grass, *Achnatherum calamagrostis*

6 *Calamagrostis acutiflora* "Karl Foerster"

7 Angelica, *Angelica archangelica*

8 Black mullein, *Verbascum nigrum*

9 *Rudbeckia fulgida* "Goldsturm"

10 *Molinia arundinacea* "Fontäne"

11 Day lily, *Hemerocallis* "Green Flutter"

12 Common yarrow, *Achillea millefolium* "Martina"

13 Tufted hair grass, *Deschampsia caespitosa* "Goldschleier"

14 Masterwort, *Astrantia major* f. *involucrata* "Canneman"

15 Day lily, *Hemerocallis citrina*

16 Hellebore, *Helleborus foetidus*

17 *Zigadenus elegans* ssp. *glaucus*

18 Lady's-mantle, *Alchemilla mollis*

19 Alumroot, *Heuchera cylindrica* "Greenfinch"

20 Needle grass, *Stipa gigantea*

21 Christmas rose, *Helleborus argutifolius*

22 Thoroughwax, *Bupleurum falcatum*

GREEN TABLE

NAME	COMMON NAME	BLOOM/ MONTHS	LIGHT	HEIGHT IN INCHES	TYPE	PLANTS PER YD²	NOTES
Acer shirasawanum "Aureum"	Japanese maple	4–5	○ ◑	to 13 ft	⚘ ✳		yellow-green leaves
Achnatherum calamagrostis		6–8	○	40–50	○	5	ornamental grass
Agropyron pubiflorum		5–7	○	10–20	○	5	grey-green ornamental grass
Amaranthus caudatus "Viridis"	Tassel flower	7–10	○	30–40	⊙	5–7	light green flowers
Ambrosinia mexicana "Green Magic"		7–9	○	30–40	⊙	9–11	green flowers
Anaphalis triplinervis	Life everlasting	6–9	○ ◑	10–20	○	5–7	grey-green leaves; white flowers
Angelica archangelica	Angelica	6–7	○ ◑	50–60	○	3	yellow-green flowers
Aquilegia viridiflora	Columbine	5–6	○ ◑	20–30	○	9	green flowers
Aristolochia macrophylla	Birthwort	6–8	○ ◑	to 33 ft	⚘	1	climber; foliage plant
Artemisia absinthium "Lambrook Silver"	Absinthe	6–9	○	20–30	○	3–5	grey-green leaves
Artemisia ludoviciana "Silver Queen"	White sage	7–8	○	30–40	○	3–5	grey-green leaves
Artemisia pontica	Sagebrush	7–8	○	30–40	○	3–5	grey-green leaves
Arundinaria murielae	Bamboo		◑	to 10 ft	⚘	1–2	
Atriplex hortensis "Gold Plume"	Garden orach	7–9	○ ◑	30–40	⊙	7–9	yellow-green leaves
Ballota pseudodictamnus		7–8	○	20–30	○	5–7	grey-green leaves; sensitive to frost
Bupleurum rotundifolium	Thoroughwax	6–8	○	10–20	⊙	5	
Buxus sempervirens	Common boxwood	4–5	○ ◑	to 4 ft	⚘	5–7	
Buxus sempervirens "Suffruticosa"	Edging boxwood		○ ◑	to 6 ft	⚘	7–9	hedgerow plant that remains low
Calamagrostis acutiflora "Karl Foerster"		7–8	○	50–60	○	3	ornamental grass
Carex pendula	Sedge grass	6	○ ◑	40–50	○	2–3	ornamental grass
Cerastium biebersteinii	Chickweed	5–6	○	12–33	○	5–7	grey-green leaves
Cynara cardunculus	Cardoon	8–9	○	60–80	○	1–2	grey-green leaves
Deschampsia caespitosa "Goldschleier"	Tufted hair grass	6–7	○ ◑	40–50	○	3–5	ornamental grass
Dryopteris filix-mas	Male fern		◑	30–50	○	5	fern
Eryngium giganteum	Eryngo	7–8	○	20–30	⊙	7	grey-green leaves
Eucomis bicolor	Pineapple lily	7–9	○	20	◉	5–7	green flowers; not winter hardy
Euphorbia amygdaloides "Purpurea"	Spurge	4–6	○ ◑	24–32	○	5–7	grey-purple leaves
Euphorbia characias wulfenii	Spurge	5–6	○	50–80	○	3–5	sensitive to frost
Euphorbia cyparissias	Cypress spurge	6–7	○ ◑	10–20	○	5–7	yellow-green
Euphorbia martinii	Spurge	4–6	○ ◑	10–20	○	5–7	sensitive to frost
Euphorbia polychroma	Spurge	5–6	○ ◑	10–20	○	5–7	yellow green
Festuca glauca "Blaufuchs"	Sheep fescue	5–6	○	10	○	9	blue-green ornamental grass
Gleditsia triacanthos inermis "Sunburst"	Honey locust	6–7	○	to 66 ft	✳		yellow-green leaves
Gunnera tinctoria		4–5	○	to 7 ft	○		foliage plant sensitive to frost
Hedera helix "Arborescens"	English ivy	8–10	○ ◑ ●	30–40	⚘	1–2	grows as a shrub
Hedera helix "Green Ripples"	English ivy	8–10	○ ◑ ●	to 26 ft	⚘	1	climber; light veins
Helianthus salicifolius	Sunflower	10	○	to 7 ft	○	5–7	beautiful leaves
Helictotrichon sempervirens		5–6	○	to 6 ft	○	7	blue-green ornamental grass
Helleborus argutifolius		3–4	○	10–20	○	7	green flowers
Helleborus foetidus	Hellebore	12–3	○	10–20	○	7	green flowers
Heuchera cylindrica "Greenfinch"	Alumroot	5–6	○ ◑	20–30	○	7	green flowers
Hosta "Krossa Regal"	Hosta	7–8	○ ◑ ●	20–30	○	1–2	blue-green leaves; purple flowers
Hosta sieboldiana "Elegans"	Plantain lily	6–7	○ ◑ ●	20–30	○	1–2	blue-green leaves
Hosta sieboldiana "Frances Williams"	Plantain lily	6–7	○ ◑ ●	20–30	○	1–2	blue-green leaves with yellow-green edge
Hosta tardiana "Blue Moon"	Hosta	7–8	○ ◑ ●	16	○	5	little blue-green leaves
Hydrangea arborescens "Grandiflora"	Hills-of-snow	7–8	○ ◑	to 10 ft	⚘		green-white flowers
Leymus arenarius			○ ◑	30–40	○	3	grey-green ornamental grass
Ligustrom ovalifolium "Aureum"	California privet	7	○ ◑	to 15 ft	⚘	3–5	yellow-green leaves
Marrubium incanum	Horehound	7–8	○	16–24	○	5	grey-green leaves
Matteuccia struthiopteris	Ostrich fern		◑ ●	40–50	○	3–5	foliage plant
Miscanthus sinensis "Malepartus"	Eulalia	8–10	○	70–80	○	1–2	ornamental grass; grey-purple panicles
Miscanthus sinensis "Undine"	Eulalia	8–10	○	80–90	○	1	ornamental grass; grey-purple panicles
Molinia arundinacea "Fontäne"		8–10	○	60–80	○	3	ornamental grass
Nicotiana langsdorffii		7–10	○ ◑	20–60	⊙	9	green flowers
Nicotiana "Lime Green"		6–10	○ ◑	20–30	⊙	9–11	green flowers
Onopordum bracteatum		8–9	○	80–100	⊙	3	grey-green leaves; violet flowers
Origanum vulgare "Tumble's Variety"	Wild marjoram	7–9	○	10–20	○	7–9	yellow-green leaves; butterfly plant
Osmunda regalis	Royal fern		○ ◑	60–80	○	3	foliage plant

144

NAME	COMMON NAME	BLOOM/ MONTHS	LIGHT	HEIGHT IN INCHES	TYPE	PLANTS PER YD²	NOTES
Pachysandra terminalis	Japanese spurge	4	◑ ◍	8–10	◍	9	evergreen ground cover
Panicum virgatum "Rehbraun"	Switch-grass	8–10	○	40–50	○	5	ornamental grass; grey-purple in autumn
Pennisetum alopecuroides "Hameln"	Chinese pennisetum	9–10	○	30–40	○	1	ornamental grass
Philadelphus coronarius "Aureus"	Mock orange	5–6	○ ◑	to 10 ft	◍		yellow-green leaves
Picea glauca "Conica"	White spruce		○ ◑	to 10 ft	◍	1	cone-shaped
Plantago major "Rosularis"	Common plantain	7–9	○ ◑	6–12	○	9–11	green leaf rosettes
Pyrus salicifolia "Pendula"	Willow-leaved pear	4–5	○	to 10 ft	◍		grey-green leaves
Reseda odorata	Common mignonette	7–9	○ ◑	10–20	◌	7–9	fragrant
Rheum palmatum	Rhubarb	6	○ ◑	to 7 ft	○	1	foliage plant
Robinia pseudoacacia "Frisia"	Black locust	6	○	to 26 ft	✱		yellow-green leaves
Rosa chinensis "Viridiflora"	China rose	6–9	○	20–30	◍	3	green flowers
Salvia argentea	Silver sage	6–7	○	20–30	⊙	7–9	grey-green leaves
Salvia officinalis "Aurea"	Common sage	6–7	○	10–20	◍	7	yellow-green leaves
Salvia officinalis "Berggarten"	Common sage	6–7	○	10–20	◍	5	grey-green leaves
Stachys byzantina "Cotton Ball"	Lamb's-ears	7–9	○	10–20	○	7	grey-green leaves
Stipa gigantea	Needle grass	7–8	○	70–90	○	2–3	ornamental grass
Taxus baccata	English yew	3–4	○ ◑	to 82 ft	◍ ✱		hedgerow plant; red fruit
Thalictrum minus "Adiantifolium"	Meadow rue	5–6	○ ◑	24–32	○	5	yellow flowers
Veratrum nigrum	False hellebore	7–8	○ ◑	40–50	○	5	foliage plant
Verbascum bombyciferum "Polarsommer"	Mullein	6–8	○ ◑	60–70	⊙	5	large grey-green leaves
Zigadenus elegans ssp. *glaucus*	White camas	7–8	○	20–30	○	7	green flowers; grey-green leaves
Zinnia elegans "Envy"	Common zinnia	6–9	○	10–20	⊙	7–9	green flowers

○ full sun; ◑ partial shade; ◍ shade
○ perennial plant; ⊙ biennial; ◌ annual; bulb; tuber; ◍ shrub; ✱ tree

When you toss a flower or some green, it is the prelude to a kiss.

The green flowers of the spurge *Euphorbia characias wulfenii* together with the purple flowers of the *Centaurea dealbata.*

COLOR
CONTRASTS

I n the preceding nine chapters, we have discussed borders planted in one color (monochrome color schemes) and those in a number of colors that are located close to each other in the color circle (analogue color schemes). Analogue colors are related to each other—they fit in well with each other and present a harmonious image. When the colors are located farther apart in the circle, a greater contrast is created.

Very significant contrasts are created by the complementary color scheme. As explained already in the introduction, this involves two colors that are located directly opposite each other in the color circle. The possibilities are: yellow and purple, yellow-orange and violet, orange and blue, orange-red and blue-green, red and green, red-purple and yellow-green. Most of the combinations of complementary colors are too intense for the garden if you use the full color in equal quantities. It is much more subtle to work with soft colors or with small accents in the complementary color.

The color directly adjacent to the complementary color also gives an exciting effect. What happens here is that, as a result of the simultaneous contrast, the color that is almost complementary will be forced towards the true complementary color. When, for example, orange is combined with violet, the orange will evoke its complementary color, blue, with the result that the violet looks bluer.

YELLOW WITH RED-PURPLE

Yellow combines excellently with red and also with purple, but the color located between these two, red-purple, is more difficult to match with yellow. Depending on the shades, the combinations may or may not be successful. As a result of the simultaneous contrast, the yellow looks greener and loses some of its brightness.

The lighter shades are the easiest to combine, for example very light yellow with tender pink. This somewhat saccharine combination is frequently seen in England, for example, in the form of yellow and light red-purple ramblers that grow intermingled against the wall of a building. There are flowers that already combine these two colors, such as many light red-purple day lilies, the annual flower-bed shrub verbena, and the annual corydalis *Corydalis sempervirens* with grey-green leaves that make a beautiful color combination with the flowers.

Dark red-purple goes well together with soft yellow, but the other way around, that is, intense yellow with light red-purple is not a very successful combination. For example, the dark red-purple masterwort *Astrantia major* "Rubra" and the green with red-purple columbine *Aquilegia vulgaris* "Nora Barlow" combine marvelously well with the soft yellow *Aquilegia chrysantha* and green-yellow *Anemone multifida*. But bright red-purple summer phloxes and intense yellow sunflowers (*Helianthus decapetalus*) together are too much of an onslaught of color.

Left
Red-purple and light yellow in Wisley Gardens, consisting of the shrub rose "F.J. Grootendorst," the day lily *Hemerocallis* "Wally Nance," *Phygelius aequalis* "Moonraker," light yellow *Chrysanthemum frutescens* "Leyton Treasure," *Penstemon* "Schoenholzen," and light yellow *Sisyrinchium striatum.*

Right
There are soft colors in this combination of yellow-green lady's-mantle and light red-purple sage (*Salvia officinalis* "Rosea").

Far right
The patio garden in the Model Gardens in light yellow, purple, and violet.

YELLOW WITH PURPLE OR VIOLET

The combination of yellow with purple or of yellow-orange with violet creates a strong contrast. These complementary colors mutually reinforce each other and, in addition, give rise to a strong light–dark contrast. Yellow is in fact the brightest color while purple has the lowest degree of brightness (see page 24). To obtain a proportionate balance between yellow and purple, one would have to use three times as much purple as yellow. Here as well, soft yellow is more beautiful than vivid yellow. In the Model Gardens at Lunteren the Patio Garden has been planted in soft yellow, yellow-green, and purple to violet; the effect is unusually beautiful. Violet garden monkshood and Canterbury bells stand next to soft yellow roses, lady's-mantle, and the yellow lupine *Lupinus* "Chandelier." A fence of black slats makes a striking background against which the colors show up

with particular clarity. In front of the entrance to her blue garden, Gertrude Jekyll had placed a yellow garden in order to prepare the eyes for the purple to blue colors (successive contrast). As a result, the purple and blue seemed brighter.

Yellow-green leaves also look beautiful together with purple and violet flowers; the yellowish leaves make the colors of the flowers extra lively. The reverse is also true since grey-purple leaves are very beautiful together with yellow flowers (see the border design on page 63).

YELLOW WITH BLUE

Together yellow and blue create a strong color-against-color contrast because they are located far away from each other in the color circle. In addition, there is a light-dark contrast since true dark blue has a low degree of brightness and seems even darker next to the bright

149

and dominant color yellow. In this combination, the beautiful color blue looks a little dull and seems to lack radiance. The situation changes when blue has the same degree of brightness as yellow, i.e., when a light shade of blue is involved. However, soft creamy yellow is most beautiful with blue flowers and it is better to avoid bright yellow. Light yellow flowers or yellow-green leaves are very subtle with light blue and perfect for a shady little corner. You can make a beautiful combination for spring with the light blue lungwort *Pulmonaria saccharata* "Cambridge Blue," light yellow comfrey *Symphytum grandiflorum* (which also exists in light blue garden varieties, such as "Hidcote Blue"), and soft yellow daffodils.

Due to the simultaneous contrast, yellow makes blue flowers seem somewhat more violet and, as a result, also a little warmer. Gertrude Jekyll liked to use small clusters of soft yellow flowers, such as the meadow rue *Thalictrum flavum*, to complete a blue border. "A blue

garden may be hungering for a group of white lilies, or for something of palest lemon-yellow," she wrote in her book about the use of color in gardens.

ORANGE WITH PURPLE OR VIOLET

A very striking color combination is orange with purple or violet. If the full colors are used, it is very loud and not too suitable for the garden, especially in the case of orange with purple. However, if light orange, light violet and grey-green leaves are selected, something very beautiful can be created. Leaves with subdued grey-

orange (brown) colors are also superb with purple or violet flowers. As a result of the simultaneous contrast, purple and violet seem bluer next to orange.

ORANGE WITH BLUE

Orange and blue are another pair of complementary colors that have a mutually reinforcing effect and can be very successful if applied well. What is important here as well is the quantity of the color that is used, for example, lots of blue with a little orange as an accent. The soft shades of orange definitely combine well with blue; but try to limit it to a few flowers. Blue is marvelous combined with grey-orange (brown); adjacent to the forceful blue, brown becomes a lively color.

You can make a double complementary color scheme by using the colors blue-green, blue, orange, and orange-red. The complementary pairs, blue/orange and blue-green/orange-red mutually reinforce each other and make this combination very exciting. In addition, a strong warm-cold contrast is created with these two warm and two cold colors. Blue-green and blue are difficult colors in which to find plants, but there is a selection available. Blue-green can be provided by the large leaves of the *Hosta sieboldiana* "Elegans" or the greyish leaves of the ornamental grass *Agropyron pubiflorum*. An example for blue is the larkspur *Delphinium* (Belladonna-hybr.) "Völkerfrieden," but violet-blue flowers also fit well into this color scheme. Orange can be found in several garden varieties of the geum, for example *Geum* "Princess Juliana." The overall picture can then be completed with the orange-red *Geum coccineum* "Feuermeer."

RED WITH VIOLET OR BLUE

Red with violet or red with blue is a very unquiet combination in the garden, certainly if pure red is used. But it is true also in this case that light shades of these colors do combine well. Light red is very romantic with light violet or light blue. The effect is about the same when light red-purple is combined with these colors. However, red is less "sugary" and conveys some warmth to the overall image.

A VARIEGATED BORDER

In a variegated border, all colors are intermingled. In such a design, attention is paid to the way in which the plants grow rather than the color of the flowers. The border design in this chapter is an example of such a variegated border. But in order to avoid clashing combinations, this design does not include vivid yellow, orange, and pure red. As can be seen, soft yellow as well as white and all the colors from red-purple to blue are represented.

The flowering periods are distributed over the entire season. Starting in March, expect the flowers of the Christmas rose and the sweet violet. The Michaelmas daisies, bugbane, and eulalia are beautiful all the way into October.

The plants are mainly perennials and, in addition, a few shrubs have been used. These are: the *Deutzia*, which is loaded with light red-purple flowers in June; the beautiful red-purple rose "Anneke Doorenbos"; the graceful *Spiraea x vanhouttei*, which bears white flowers; and the jasmine "Dame Blanche" with its delightful fragrance. Make the overall image more interesting by adding beautiful bulbs and annuals.

On the right-hand side of the border is a corner that juts inward; a shed or a corner of the house could be located there. The layout of the plants is such that next to this wall are plants that can grow in half shade. The remainder of the border needs to be fully exposed to the sun. Against the wall are two climbing plants, a honeysuckle and a *Clematis*. These climbers, which do need to have an extra support, provide a beautiful background.

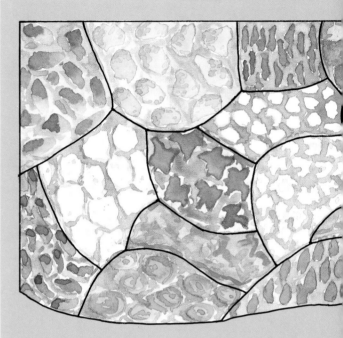

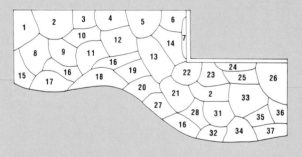

1 Purple oregano, *Origanum laevigatum* "Herrenhausen"

2 Stephanotis, *Deutzia hybrida* "Contraste"

3 Speedwell, *Veronica virginica*

4 Larkspur, *Delphinium* "Gletscherwasser"

5 Eulalia, *Miscanthus sinensis* "Malepartus"

6 Queen-of-the-prairie, *Filipendula rubra* "Venusta Magnifica"

7 Virgin's bower, *Clematis* "The President"

8 Gypsophila, *Gypsophila paniculata*

9 Bergamot, *Monarda* "Kardinal"

10 Japanese anemone, *Anemone x hybrida* "Honorine Jobert"

11 Masterwort, *Astrantia major* "Margery Fish"

12 Sage, *Salvia nemorosa* "Tänzerin"

13 Cow parsnip, *Acanthus mollis*

Variegated in Plant Names

bicolor—two-color
pictus—variegated
polychroma—polychrome
psittacina—as variegated as a parrot
quadricolor—four-color
tricolor—three-color

DESIGN AND LIST OF PLANTS

Design: Modeste Herwig. Measurements: 30 × 13 ft. (9 × 4 m.)

14 Michaelmas daisy, *Aster novi-belgii* "Climax"

15 Germander, *Teucrium marum*

16 Artemisia, *Artemisia ludoviciana* "Silver Queen"

17 *Rosa* "Anneke Doorenbos"

18 Catmint, *Nepeta x faassenii*

19 Bellflower, *Campanula lactiflora* "Pouffe"

20 Lady's-mantle, *Alchemilla mollis*

21 Common yarrow, *Achillea millefolium* "Hoffnung"

22 Spirea, *Spiraea vanhouttei*

23 Red turtlehead, *Chelone obliqua*

24 Honeysuckle, *Lonicera periclymenum*

25 Bugbane, *Cimicifuga simplex* "White Pearl"

26 Jasmine, *Philadelphus* "Dame Blanche"

27 Mountain bluet, *Centaurea montana*

28 Skullcap, *Scutellaria incana*

29 *Eryngium planum*

30 Meadow rue, *Thalictrum aquilegifolium*

31 Musk mallow, *Malva moschata* "Alba"

32 *Geranium sylvaticum* "Mayflower"

33 Crane's bill, *Geranium* "Johnson's Blue"

34 Globe-flower, *Trollius* "Earliest of All"

35 Christmas rose, *Helleborus orientalis*

36 Sweet pea, *Lathyrus vernus*

37 Sweet violet, *Viola odorata*

PHOTO CREDITS

Metric Equivalents

INCHES TO MILLIMETRES AND CENTIMETRES

MM—millimetres   CM—centimetres

Inches	MM	CM	Inches	CM	Inches	CM
⅛	3	0.3	9	22.9	30	76.2
¼	6	0.6	10	25.4	31	78.7
⅜	10	1.0	11	27.9	32	81.3
½	13	1.3	12	30.5	33	83.8
⅝	16	1.6	13	33.0	34	86.4
¾	19	1.9	14	35.6	35	88.9
⅞	22	2.2	15	38.1	36	91.4
1	25	2.5	16	40.6	37	94.0
1¼	32	3.2	17	43.2	38	96.5
1½	38	3.8	18	45.7	39	99.1
1¾	44	4.4	19	48.3	40	101.6
2	51	5.1	20	50.8	41	104.1
2½	64	6.4	21	53.3	42	106.7
3	76	7.6	22	55.9	43	109.2
3½	89	8.9	23	58.4	44	111.8
4	102	10.2	24	61.0	45	114.3
4½	114	11.4	25	63.5	46	116.8
5	127	12.7	26	66.0	47	119.4
6	152	15.2	27	68.6	48	121.9
7	178	17.8	28	71.1	49	124.5
8	203	20.3	29	73.7	50	127.0

INDEX

155